UNLOCK YOUR GREATNESS IN SEVEN DAYS

A Transformational Journey to Unleash Your Authentic Power

Dr Sylvia Forchap- Likambi

Copyright ©2025 by Dr Sylvia Forchap-Likambi

ISBN-13: 978-1-913266-32-5

All rights reserved. No part of this book may be reproduced or transmitted in any form or by any means, electronic or mechanical, including photocopying, recording, or by an information storage and retrieval system – except by a reviewer who may quote brief passages in a review to be printed in a magazine or newspaper – without permission in writing from the copyright owner.

Other books by the Author:

The Supreme Law of Gratitude: The Ultimate Antidote for Grief

ISBN-13: 978-1-913266-31-8

Visionary Woman: Moved by Purpose, Not by Sight

ISBN-13: 978-1-913266-09-7

Personal & Professional Transformation and Success Planner: Your Blueprint to Success & Abundance in All Areas of Your Life – Parts one and two

ISBN-13: 978-1-913266-08-0

Unleash Your Authentic Identity: Unlock Your True Identity & Purpose

ISBN-13: 978-1-913266-95-0

Success Blueprint: Timeless Principles to Enable You to Identify & Accomplish True Success & Fulfilment in All Areas of Life

ISBN-13: 978-1-913266-98-1

Principles of Resolution: A Practical Step-by-Step Guide to Enable You to Identify, Set & Accomplish Your Goals

ISBN 10: 1543063780

ISBN13:9781543063783

Seven Powerful Strategies for Overcoming Life Challenges: Tested & Proven Life-Changing Keys

ISBN-13: 978-1-913266-02-8

ISBN-10: 1975669584

A Father's Tender and Compassionate Love: A Love So Tender, Compassionate, and Unconditional

ISBN 10: 1479772887/ ISBN 13: 9781479772889

ISBN 10: 1479772879 ISBN/ 13: 9781479772872

DEDICATION

To those who dare to dream,
To those who believe in the greatness within,
To the seekers of purpose,
And the warriors of resilience,

This book is for you.

May you recognise the boundless potential within your soul and step boldly into the greatness that is your birthright. May your journey be one of self-discovery, empowerment, and transformation.

For all those who have walked alongside me, who have inspired, supported, and encouraged me—this is as much your journey as it is mine. Your unwavering belief in me has made this work possible.

With deepest gratitude and love,
Dr Sylvia Forchap-Likambi

Table of Contents

How To Read This Book 1

Preface 5

Day 1 – Identifying Your Seed of Greatness 9

Day 2 – Visualising Your Greatness: Breaking Free from Limitations 19

Day 3 – Unveiling Your Unique Vision 37

Day 4 – Unlock the Transformational Power of Your Mind 55

Day 5 – Affirming Your Greatness: Awakening the Power Within 67

Day 6 – Anchored in Purpose: Standing Firm in Your Convictions 77

Day 7 – Unlocking the Gateway to Your Greatness 97

About Dr Sylvia Forchap-Likambi 113

How To Read This Book

In this section, I would like to offer some guidance on reading this book to get the most out of it.

This book is your unique blueprint and roadmap to unlocking your greatness. To gain the most from its pages, follow these simple instructions, keeping in mind the author's authentic, straightforward style:

1. **Read Gradually**
   This is not a book to rush through or skim. It is designed to be read gradually over seven days. Each day represents a chapter of the book and marks a step on your transformational journey.

2. **Allocate Time Each Day**
   Dedicate time each day to fully immerse yourself in one chapter. Read thoughtfully and reflect deeply on the wisdom and guidance shared. Let each chapter resonate with you, one day at a time.

3. **Reflect and Absorb**

   After reading a chapter, reflect on its key messages. Apply the principles to your life and allow them to shape your beliefs, values, thoughts, mindset, and actions.

4. **Embrace the Journey**

   Treat these seven days as a journey of self-discovery and transformation. Engage actively, and take the time to understand and internalise the lessons as they unfold daily.

5. **Return for Guidance**

   Whether you have completed a single day or the full seven-day journey, this book remains a trusted companion. Revisit it in times of uncertainty or overwhelm or whenever you need clarity, guidance, and confidence to move forward.

6. **Commit to Your Growth**

   Commit to reading and re-reading the book as needed. Use it as inspiration, motivation, and wisdom throughout your journey toward greatness.

By dedicating just seven days and being willing to reflect, learn, and grow, you will undoubtedly unlock powerful insights and divine wisdom that will inspire and empower you to embrace your uniqueness and greatness.

At the end of the seven days, you are invited to consult the book in times of uncertainty or overwhelm or simply for guidance and confidence as you journey towards greatness.

Preface

"Noble and great. Courageous and determined. Faithful and fearless. That is who you are and who you have always been. Understanding this can change your life, for this knowledge carries a confidence that cannot be replicated in any other way."
— Sheri Dew

By reading this book, you are embarking on a journey to unlock the greatness within you. But first, you must be aware that greatness resides in you. Without awareness, it is impossible to unlock your potential and greatness, for you cannot access what you are unaware of or do not acknowledge. Awareness is the first step towards transformation. So, as you begin this journey with me, I trust you already know, even if you've never truly experienced it, that greatness lies within you. You may not have seen it before, but I believe you know it's there, waiting to be awakened.

Many of us remain unaware of the greatness within, living in a state of ignorance that keeps us trapped in mediocrity. As Hosea 4:6

reminds us, "My people perish for lack of knowledge." Too many people today remain disadvantaged because they have been deprived of knowledge—the knowledge of their power, potential, and purpose. If you do not know who you are and what you are capable of, you will settle for a life far below your true potential. Knowledge is potential power; the first step toward unlocking your greatness is understanding who you truly are.

To live a life of purpose, fulfilment, and greatness, you must return to the basics of self-awareness. You must ask yourself profound questions: Who are you? Why were you born? Why are you here? What is your purpose? Where are you going? What will you do when you reach your destination? And how will it feel? The answers to these questions mark the beginning of your journey of self-discovery as you uncover the greatness within you—revealing it to yourself and the world.

The greatness within you is crying out to be released. It is not meant to be contained. Just as a seed carries the potential to grow into something magnificent and beautiful, the greatness within you is waiting to be nurtured so it can blossom into the fruit of your purpose. This greatness is not visible yet—it is hidden in the seed of potential within you. If you are not spiritually connected to the divine power within, you may struggle to see, understand, or even believe it's there.

Our journey begins with the seed—the seed of greatness that lies within us. Take a moment to imagine a seed you love—perhaps the familiar orange seed. Within that tiny seed is the potential for an entire tree, with branches bearing countless oranges. These oranges were never external; they were already encoded in the seed. Similarly, within your DNA, a unique blueprint was created at conception. This blueprint defines who you are and who you are meant to become. From that very moment, you were destined for greatness.

Everything God creates is made with purpose. He is the source of greatness, and His image is embedded in every creation, including you and me. Like the orange seed, your greatness is encoded within your being. As the seed is nurtured, it grows into a tree that produces fruit. Just as the tree bears fruit for all to benefit from, so will you fulfil your purpose, touching lives and offering your unique gifts to the world.

Now, I ask you: Are you ready to unlock your greatness? Are you ready to uncover the potential encoded in your very DNA? Science may never be able to explain this, but your Creator, the one who placed this greatness within you, knows exactly what it is. No one could have known the greatness that would emerge from that tiny seed—fetus, from that moment of conception.

You are a masterpiece, an original creation destined for greatness. No one could understand your full potential when you were conceived or as you grew up in your mother's womb. But now, as you mature, you are beginning to realise it. It is time for you to uncover the greatness within, embrace your unique purpose, and start the journey of bringing that greatness to fruition.

The greatness within you is not determined by how you look, where you come from, or your financial status. Your educational background or your gender does not define it. It is spiritual, intangible, and infinite. It is a mystery only God truly knows, and He has concealed it for your protection. Why? Because if others knew your potential before you were ready to handle it, they might crush it before it had the chance to develop and flourish.

This is why your greatness is hidden—because it's not time for it to be revealed. The key is that when the moment or season comes for you to understand and unlock it, you will be mature enough to protect and preserve it. You will know that this greatness is your birthright, and you will be ready to claim, nurture, and bring it to the world. It is your unique purpose on Earth.

Now, the time has come, which is why you are reading this book. You are ready to take control of your greatness, to embrace it fully and protect it fiercely. You are prepared to nurture it, grow it, and see it manifest and blossom. Welcome to your journey of greatness. This is where it all begins.

DAY ONE

Identifying Your Seed of Greatness

"Integrity is the first step to true greatness."
– Charles Simmons

Awakening Your Inner Power

Welcome to day one of your transformational journey to unlocking your greatness with Dr Sylvia Forchap-Likambi. You are indeed great and already have a seed of greatness within you. Let us begin this journey by discovering that seed. What kind of seed are you? You will naturally flourish most authentically once you identify your seed of greatness. There will be no struggle—just as an orange seed effortlessly grows into an orange tree and bears oranges.

Although you might resemble those around you—your peers, family, or community—you are not the same; you are unique. Imagine an orange seed, a lemon seed, a grapefruit seed, and a tangerine seed. Four seeds—orange, lemon, grapefruit, and tangerine. Don't they look so alike? If we placed all these seeds into one box, most people would think they were identical. They might label them as the same or group them into one category— "citrus fruits." In the same way, society often puts us into a box and labels us. Perhaps you've been defined by your skin colour, your gender, your nationality, or your financial status. Your marital status might have even labelled you—whether single, married, or a single parent raising children alone.

Maybe you have defined yourself this way because you appear similar to others. But as you embark on this journey to greatness, it's time to distinguish yourself. It's time to recognise where you truly stand among the crowd. Today marks a new beginning—the day you identify your uniqueness and differentiate yourself. Are you an orange seed? A lemon seed? A grapefruit seed? A tangerine seed?

Take control and ownership of your identity. Don't let others define you; most people cannot see the difference. Only those with deep insight—experts in agriculture, for instance—can recognise the uniqueness of each seed, even at its earliest stage.

Similarly, it takes a special kind of insight and divine wisdom to see the greatness within you when it is not yet fully visible. That is why you are on this journey with someone like me—a mindset transformation coach and a leading empowerment and transformation authority—who can see the difference even in your darkest hour.

Where others define you by your dim light or even the absence of it, I see the light in you. Even when you are engulfed in darkness, I can see your light. And I am here to help extract it, to pull that light out of you and unveil it so you can unlock your greatness. Together, we will remove the veil covering your greatness and obscuring your light. You will step into the glory of God, and that glory will manifest and reveal itself in you.

Welcome to your greatness. It doesn't have to be grand at the start—remember, it is a seed. The seed is often the smallest part of the fruit, hidden within it. The fruit itself is far greater than the seed it came from. Greatness frequently starts small, like DNA—so complex and microscopic that it cannot be deciphered or seen with the naked eye. Your greatness, encoded within you, is invisible to many who lack insight and the vision to see beyond. Those who cannot see the essence of greatness within you may treat you like an ordinary person. They may go about their lives unaware of the brilliance that resides within you. But this does not diminish your greatness. You are entrusted with nurturing this seed, bringing it to life, and allowing it to grow into a thriving tree of greatness that bears abundant fruit.

Are you ready to nurture that greatness, to bring it to life? Are you ready to give birth to the tiny light within you? To sow the seed of greatness inside you, watch it grow into a mighty tree, and bear incredible fruits of greatness?

By your fruits, people will come to know you. They will recognise your deeds and actions of greatness and see who you truly are. By then, it will be undeniable—the fruits of your greatness will already be evident.

And remember this: every fruit you produce contains seeds and every action you take sows the seeds of future greatness. These seeds will continue to grow, bear more fruit, and leave a lasting legacy.

So, what seed are you? What do you love to do naturally? What do you see yourself becoming naturally? What brings you joy effortlessly, whether under pressure or no pressure? What is your natural inclination in life?

Are you ready to take this seed of greatness to the world? To make the decision that you will assert and recognise the seed of greatness that lies within you? Once you recognise and acknowledge this seed of greatness within, you instantly gain knowledge—and knowledge is the beginning of every transformational journey. However, applying the knowledge—wisdom—holds power and will transform your life as you embark on this journey of unlocking your greatness.

Before we proceed any further, I want you to make a pledge to yourself and confess these words:

"I am willing to take this seed of greatness, which I know lies within me, and sow it. I am ready to embrace wisdom—to sow this seed and to invest in its potential. I will nurture and feed it day and night until it takes root, breaks through the soil, and begins to grow.

When it starts to grow, I am prepared to continue nurturing it, protecting it, and eradicating pests. I will build a fence around my garden to preserve it, keep thieves from stealing it, and prevent others from destroying it or trampling it. I am ready to safeguard this garden where my greatness is sown.

I understand the need for action, for I have learnt that knowledge alone does not bring about change. Transformation comes only through the wisdom of applying the knowledge gained in the relevant areas of my life so that its effects may become evident and manifest.

I am ready to step into this journey. I am ready to take action—yes! Yes! Yes! I am ready to act. I am so excited about this seed because I know it is not ordinary. I know it is not something that others can readily see or recognise. Only my Creator, who knows what is encoded and entrapped within my DNA, and I, who have been given ownership and custodianship over this seed, can truly comprehend its value.

I know and am ready to take full advantage of my seed. I will utilise this seed to its full potential. I will exercise the authority and power granted to me, sow this seed today, and begin letting the greatness within it sprout. I am ready to see the seed take root, sprout, grow, and produce fruits of greatness. Yes, I am!"

But before you decide to sow the seed of greatness in you—you must take a moment to reflect. You cannot sow and elevate your life blindly. I want you to truly understand the seed of greatness within and the fruit that you so deeply desire to become—because once you sow your seed of greatness, it will start growing, and it is bound to produce the fruits that are entrapped within.

If you have a specific desire, God has placed it within you to envisage and experience. That desire is the greatness—the fruit—you are born to become. So, you must uncover what you desire, not what your mother or your father desires, not what your spouse or society desires, or what they have told you to desire.

Take some time today, on day one, to list and write down your heart's desires. What type of fruit do you want to reap? The harvest does not determine the fruit—the seed does. The seed determines the fruit. Hence, you automatically recognise the seed you want to sow by identifying the type of fruit you would love to reap. Therefore, as you embark on this journey of sowing, you must be very sure of the type of fruit you wish to harvest. What kind of fruit do you truly desire, the fruit that, when you consume it or share it with others, will make you feel fulfilled, nourished, and accomplished? What is that fruit? What do you long to become?

You cannot desire to reap oranges and yet sow a lemon seed. You cannot dream of harvesting mangoes if you sow an apple seed. So, choose wisely. Choose the seed that will produce the fruit you desire to reap. Choose the fruit of greatness you wish to become and share with the world. I repeat, choose the fruit of greatness—choose well.

Take your time. Reflect. Reflect deeply.

You might desire something that no one in your neighbourhood or family has ever desired, and that's okay. It's more than OK—it's extraordinary. That desire was placed uniquely within you. Remember, while you might look like everyone else, you may come from the same family—the "citrus family," so to speak—you might be a lemon, not an orange. You might be a grapefruit, not a tangerine.

Do not choose based on what looks familiar or what others around you have done. Instead, follow your natural inclinations and your heart's deepest desires. Choose to become what you yearn for and aspire to be. That desire was placed within you for a reason.

How do you long for something you have never seen? Because it already exists within you. It is encoded in your DNA. It is your unique blueprint of greatness. That's why you desire it.

What are your heart's desires? What fruits do you wish to reap? What are the fruits you genuinely desire to reap?

You cannot desire to reap peace yet choose to sow unrest, strife, or conflict. You cannot hope to reap love while sowing hatred or malice. You cannot desire to reap forgiveness yet choose to sow unforgiveness. You cannot hope for joy while sowing sadness and melancholy. You cannot desire to reap optimism but sow seeds of pessimism. You cannot wish to reap positivity yet choose to sow negativity.

Choose your seed wisely.

Remember, this is the beginning of your transformational journey—day one. Take the time to discover the seeds you want to sow that will yield the fruits you long to reap.

Now, you should already know what these fruits look like. Use all your senses to connect with them. You should know how these fruits taste, how they look, and how they feel. You must understand the pleasure and satisfaction they bring when you see or experience them. You must know the fulfilment and joy they provide when you consume them.

Use your senses to envision your desired greatness. See, feel, and imagine the joy and fulfilment it will bring. Picture yourself living this life of greatness. Your vision will guide you, for you can only achieve what you can see. Open the eyes of your heart and visualise your destiny. What do you see? What greatness lies ahead of you? By the end of this year, what is the greatness you envision? What is the greatness you feel? What is the life you yearn for? What emotions stir powerfully within you, lighting up your soul like lightning?

See it. Feel it. Touch it.

We cannot reach out for what we cannot see. You can only go as far as your vision allows. Once again, open your eyes—the eyes of your heart, your spiritual eyes. See it. Feel it. Imagine it. Visualise that fruit you desire, that life you long to live.

And as you do, I want you to focus on how you will feel when you live this life. Picture yourself in that moment.

Tomorrow, we will step into day two of this transformational journey to unlocking your greatness. Welcome aboard this journey to unlocking your greatness. Thank you for your time and cooperation, and I look forward to seeing you tomorrow. On day two, we will begin visualising this seed of greatness.

Remember: farmers never sow without preparation. There is always a moment of preparation—a time to gather the best seeds—to separate the good from the bad. They carefully choose the seeds they desire; sometimes, they travel great distances to obtain them. In the same way, you must journey deep within—beyond the physical realm—into your spirit and soul. Connect with the divine. Align with God's purpose for your life. Tap into the divine power to uncover the seed of greatness placed within you.

As you discover and sow this seed, you will step into your greatness this year and in the future.

DAY TWO

Visualising Your Greatness: Breaking Free from Limitations

"If any man seeks for greatness, let him forget greatness and ask for truth, and he will find both."
– Horace Mann

Welcome to Day Two of your transformational journey to unlocking your greatness. Together, we are embarking on this incredible journey, and today, we delve deeper into uncovering and embracing the greatness within you.

Let's briefly reflect on Day One. You realise you are inherently incredible, born with a seed of greatness. This seed lies within you, waiting to be uncovered, unlocked, and nurtured so you can walk fully in your greatness. Remember, the seed determines the harvest—nothing else.

On Day One, we focused on recognising this seed of greatness. I asked you to imagine that you have been given a garden, and it is your responsibility to sow the seeds you love and desire to see flourish in your life. What seeds have you chosen?

These seeds must align with what you truly love. As we explored, an orange seed will naturally grow into an orange tree and produce oranges without struggle. Similarly, a tangerine seed will produce tangerines effortlessly. Your desires are like those seeds. The very fact that you desire to be someone, achieve something, or accomplish a particular goal is evidence of the greatness placed within you at creation. You will naturally grow to become what you were designed to be.

However, too often, we limit ourselves. We constrain our desires and dreams within the boundaries of our current circumstances, conditions, or identities—be it our skin colour, financial status, or societal expectations. We place our aspirations in a box, restricting our imagination and preventing ourselves from dreaming beyond the scope of our present reality.

On Day Two, I want you to break free. Let this day mark the beginning of your journey to freedom—stepping outside any box, situation, or circumstance that has held you back. Today, we embark on a journey of visualisation that takes you beyond every barrier, limitation, and current condition.

This is your moment to be free. It is time to let every chain be loosened, every door of possibility flung open. The greatness within you is waiting to emerge, and your deepest desires are ready to be unlocked.

On this second day, we focus on liberating your mind and spirit. This is the day you begin visualising the life you deserve—a life of greatness, joy, fulfilment, and abundance. This is your birthright. You were born to live an extraordinary life. Anything less is settling for mediocrity, which has no place in your story. You were never born to live an average life. You were born to thrive and flourish in greatness.

You were born to soar like an eagle—to rise to greater heights. However, you can only soar as far as you can see. Always remember: your journey in life will only take you as far as your vision allows. Yet, with the power of visualisation, you can transcend the physical limitations of sight, which is merely a function of the eyes. Now, we will move beyond those barriers. Together, we will look into your heart and mind, embarking on an eternal, timeless, limitless, infinite journey.

I want you to take a moment now—wherever you are. Sit down, relax, or lie down. This is Day Two of your journey, a significant step in unlocking the greatness that lies within you. Choose a time and space where you are calm and undistracted for the best results. The ideal environment for this exercise is one where you feel completely at peace—a place that lets you let go of all tension and feel at ease. If you are occupied with something else, I encourage you to pause and find a tranquil setting to continue.

When you're ready, find a comfortable position—sitting or lying down. Let us begin this transformational journey of visualising the greatness within you, waiting to be unveiled, unlocked, and released.

Start by relaxing your shoulders. Drop them completely—release any tension you may be holding. If you are wearing shoes, consider taking them off to feel even more comfortable. Now, let's bring relaxation to your entire body, starting at the top of your head and working down to the soles of your feet.

Relax the muscles in your head and face. Let your forehead smooth out. Don't frown; don't crease your face. Let your facial muscles rest naturally—serene, calm, and plain. If you feel like smiling, that's fine, but there's no need to force it. Let your jaw loosen and drop slightly. Close your eyes gently, and let everything settle into a state of relaxation.

Now, let your ears relax. Ease any tension in your neck. You might roll your neck gently from side to side. Change direction, tilting your head forward and backwards, loosening any tightness. Stretch your neck muscles lightly, and then let them relax. If you're lying down, sink into the surface beneath you and close your eyes.

Take a deep breath. Breathe slowly and deeply, becoming fully aware of the air entering your nostrils and flowing into your lungs. Visualise this process: the air travelling through your nostrils, down your trachea, and filling your lungs. Hold your breath for a moment, then exhale gently. Feel the tension leaving your body with each breath. Drop your shoulders again, and let yourself relax completely.

This is your moment. Let go of all distractions and tension. Focus on the present, and prepare yourself to see, feel, and embrace the greatness within you. Breathe out and relax. Drop your shoulders as you breathe out.

Let's do this again: breathe in gently and slowly, keeping a relaxed facial expression. Follow the air as it moves through your nostrils and into your lungs. Relax your muscles. Hold your breath for a moment, then exhale.

Take another deep breath—this time more profound than before. Feel the air filling your lungs, pushing against your diaphragm. Hold it briefly, then exhale fully. You may expel the air through your mouth if you prefer. Now, take another deep breath, then breathe out and relax.

Let your hands and fingers loosen entirely. Allow them to be fully at ease. Give your fingers a slight shake to ensure they are entirely relaxed. Let your hands rest naturally, either by your side or on the bed if you're lying down.

Now, bring your attention to your legs. Relax your knees down to the soles of your feet. Let your toes release any tension—don't strain or move them. Let them rest.

If you're sitting, let your feet rest naturally against the floor or the edge of your chair. If you're lying down, allow your entire body to sink into the surface beneath you. Relax completely.

Take another deep breath. Hold it. Then exhale, expelling the air through your mouth. Once more, breathe deeply, hold it for a moment, and breathe out. Don't let your mind wander to anything else—focus on your breath. Follow the air as it enters your nostrils and flows into your lungs.

Now, in this calm state, whisper to yourself:
"I surrender. I surrender all my thoughts, worries, and negativity."

Let these words flow naturally from within. Place yourself in complete surrender—letting go of control, allowing worries and concerns to dissipate. Release the thoughts that clutter your mind. Surrender entirely to the divine, to your Creator—God. Surrender your pains, troubles, trials, and limitations. Let go of the obstacles and barriers that have held you back.

Take a deep breath and relax further. Now, picture a whiteboard—a completely blank, white surface standing in front of you. As you breathe in and out, focus on this whiteboard. It is pure and empty, untouched.

This whiteboard represents the year 2025 or another year in the future of your choice—a brand-new year. Nothing is yet written upon it: no stories, no mistakes, no successes, no failures. This year is an unwritten chapter. It marks the beginning of the year—a new year and era.

No one has lived this year before—it is uniquely yours to shape. This year, this journey is a fresh start. If you embarked on this journey at the beginning of the year, then today marks the second day of your path to unlocking the greatness within you. The whiteboard before you symbolises a new page, a fresh chapter in your unfolding story. It also represents a new life, opportunity, and day—the days ahead remain unknown. You haven't experienced this day yet, nor do you know what it holds.

All you know is that it is a new day, full of possibilities and opportunities, waiting for you to embrace and project the results and fruits you want to reap. In a nutshell, this is what this board represents—an empty board—a whiteboard. It symbolises purity and clarity. It holds nothing—no past mistakes, no regrets, no expectations.

Now, I want you to project what you want and desire onto this board. What do you want? What do you desire for yourself? By the end of this journey, whether in seven days or by the end of 2025 or another year. Remember, this blank board is here for you. You have the authority; you have complete control over it. No one has marked it; no one has written on it. There are no regrets, no expectations. This is for you to write. Write your story. Write the life you want to live. Write the life you desire to live.

Remember that someone else will if you don't write anything on this board because it is free and available. If someone else sees this blank space and has a vision—so many goals and ambitions — they will fill it in. They will write on it if you don't decide what life you want to live. The board is free; it is unused and available for use. Hence, if you don't live your desired life, someone else will prescribe or dictate that life for you.

Someone will give you a life. Society will, your parents, your spouse, your friends—they will decide for you. This board, this blank space, is meant to be filled. It's not meant to stay blank. It must be used – either by you or by someone else. If you don't use it, if you don't write your story, if you don't write about the life you want to live, someone else will do it for you and hand it over to you. You will then be forced to live the life they have written on their terms, not yours. What a tragedy. What a great tragedy that would be.

So, it is wise for you to make use of it. If you don't know what to write, do not worry. Just leave it blank for the moment until after this exercise or later. Or if you've written something on it, and after this visualisation exercise, you realise that what you wrote needs to change, that's fine. It's allowed. Life is flexible. This is your vision board; it is blank. You can write what you want and draw what you want. If you don't like the story you've written, you can change it.

Don't worry if you don't like what you want to achieve or feel you've limited yourself; it can evolve later. But if you know what you want now and set it out, you will have a greater chance of living a well-planned and successful life.

So, as you sit back or lie down, I want you to breathe in again and envision this blank screen or board in front of you. Imagine what might be occurring in your life right now. You may face challenges, health issues, or doubts as you read these words. Now, I want you to imagine being on a beautiful, peaceful beach near the ocean if you love the sea. Imagine the wind and the waves carrying away all your trials, all your tribulations, and all your shortcomings. If your challenge is poor health, imagine it being blown away by the wind and sea waves—never to return. Every ailment, every health concern you have is carried away. You are being replenished with good health. You are refreshed and revived through the breeze of life that's blowing over you. Your pain, sorrow, and heartache are swept away by this ocean, by this wave, never to return.

If your struggle is with finances, perhaps you're in debt; I want you to imagine all of it being carried away. A fresh wind, a fresh breeze, bringing you all the wealth and much more than you've ever desired in your lifetime. Picture it—a wind of prosperity coming over you. You have millions; you have food; you have abundance. Money is no longer a problem. You possess such immense wealth that it flows towards you like a never-ending stream, brought by the ocean, by the waves. So much prosperity, so many resources, so much wealth – you are now in a better place. You have more than enough—than you ever dreamed of in your lifetime. You are overflowing. It's spilling over, flowing from the overflow. You have enough to fill yourself up and still give to others.

All your debt is settled, and now you live in abundance.

If your problem is homelessness, imagine this wind bringing you villas upon villas. You now own more than enough homes. You're living in a mansion you never dreamed of—not just one mansion, but many. You are now the proud owner of a huge complex. You are a landlord with countless properties. Homelessness is no longer your problem—you have more than enough houses for yourself and others.

I want you to take another deep breath and relax in this state. If your problem lies in your marriage or relationship – perhaps you've faced abuse or hard times—I want you to imagine the dysfunction being washed away. Forgiveness comes in abundance. Joy returns to your marriage; your relationship is restored. A wind of restoration is blowing over you. Blowing onto you is a fresh breeze, carrying waves of love, peace, joy, and happiness.

Picture your home filled with so much peace. The past, with all its pain and oppression—whether it's a friend or a toxic relationship—is being carried away by this wind, by this ocean, never to return. Your life is now transformed, brimming with great relationships and surrounded by people who love, cherish, and admire you.

The ocean pours over you in waves of love, mercy, and grace. A love so profound, so extraordinary, it feels almost unreal. A love you've never experienced before. Not because you earned it but because you were chosen to receive it. Because you are unique. You are special.

And whatever has been oppressing you—whether it's a parent, an employer, or someone else —I want you to imagine this wind carrying them away, once and for all. Your life is restored with the best relationships, the finest employers, and supportive bosses and colleagues. People who love, respect, cherish, and esteem you. I want you to imagine all your pains being swept away by this wind, never to return.

Whatever your problem maybe—if it's childlessness, if you've thought of yourself as barren—now see yourself as the mother of nations. Picture these amazing children, all yours, and grandchildren too. Imagine a wave of fertility washing over you, a wind of fruitfulness.

You are so blessed that you cry out joyfully because you have many wonderful children who love and cherish you. You are overwhelmed, conceiving every year and giving birth to beautiful sons and daughters. You see generations of grandchildren surrounding you, bringing light and love into your life. Imagine all your past pain swept away by this wave, carried by this wind, never to return. Your life is full of joy, prosperity, great love, fertility, abundance, peace, and financial blessings.

Imagine having everything—much more than you could have ever desired. You have everything: homes, cars, money, finances, children, and extraordinary relationships. More than you ever thought possible. You now lack nothing.

If you have been struggling with immigration issues, see yourself standing in a new country or in the country where you are seeking refuge. Imagine being granted your citizenship. This wind is carrying your new status to you—you are now a citizen of that nation. Where once you were an asylum seeker or refugee, now you belong. You are a citizen, entitled to every right that citizenship provides. And above all, you are a citizen of the kingdom of heaven, embraced and cherished.

Now, as you sit back, you realise you lack nothing. Your life is abundant in every area: health, career, finances, relationships, personal growth, and spiritual connection. You experience a profound bond with the divine. You feel like a child of God, deeply loved and cherished. His warmth and presence surround you. You sense His greatness and His mighty protection over your life. You are sheltered, secure, and at peace.

As you sit relaxed in this moment of abundance, take a deep breath. Breathe in the breath of life. Breathe out, and feel the peace within you. In this state of contentment, with the whiteboard in front of you, remember: you lack nothing. Your mindset is now one of abundance—of love, prosperity, fulfilment, and friendship, and you have everything you've ever dreamt of having on this earth.

Look at that board right now. If I were to ask you, what do you desire now? Who do you see yourself becoming? Remember, you are no longer working to pay bills or meet ends. You have an abundance of wealth and lack nothing.

So, what would you do with your life? What do you desire to do right now? How do you envision your mornings, your days, and your steps? What life do you desire to live? Look at that board, and let your imagination stretch as far as it can go. Picture the life you truly want. Use all your senses:

See it. What does it look like?
Hear it. What does it sound like?
Perceive it. What does it smell like?
Feel it. How does it touch you?

How does it feel to live the life of your dreams? Now that there are no limitations and you have everything in abundance, what is it that you genuinely desire to become?

Can you see the person you are becoming? Can you envision that individual? What do they look like? Can you feel their presence? What does it feel like to be that extraordinary person you desire to become? What do you think? What do you see? What can you touch? What can you smell around you as this individual living the life you deserve?

Imagine touching that life now, reaching out and holding it as if it's real. How does it feel? Can you see the life you yearn for? The life you've always dreamed of, free from physical limitations? Because now, you're looking beyond the barriers of your current reality.

Beyond what your physical eyes can see, you are forming a vivid mental picture of your ideal life.

This is the life you desire, without challenges or shortcomings. You are seeing beyond your present circumstances, beyond your finances. You are creating a mental picture of your purpose. If you can visualise this life, it is because it has already been deposited within you by God. You can now sense the greatness inside you, waiting to unfold. It's natural for this greatness to emerge and grow when unhindered.

This is who you are destined to become. This is the life you are destined to live. This is how you will feel—fulfilled, at peace, and alive with purpose. That seed of greatness is already within you. Hold on to it. Nurture it. This is your life, your greatness, your power, your purpose.

Purpose transcends the mundane. It goes beyond working to pay mortgages or striving to make ends meet. The purpose is bigger than living out of fear. Living with purpose brings a profound sense of fulfilment, achievement, accomplishment, peace, and rest. Can you feel it now? Can you sense that deep, satisfying peace within you? The sense of "Wow, I made it"?

This is the life you've always yearned for. The life you love. The life that will yield abundant fruit—not just for yourself, but for your world, for generations to come. This life will leave a lasting legacy and glorify your Father in heaven. This is the very reason you were born.

Now, I want you to write on that board. Write your story. This is the seed of your greatness. The seed you are going to plant. As you prepare for the sowing, remember that your visualisation has lifted you beyond the limitations of your heart, your gender, your race, your religion, your skin colour, and your environment.

It has taken you into the realm of the divine—God, the Creator. In this place, you can see the life He designed for you and desires you to live. Go forth and embrace this life.

So, what is that life? What does it look like? This is your seed of greatness, and we will work on unveiling and unlocking it. When it begins to sprout and grow, it will produce the fruit of greatness hidden within it all along.

Remember, every fruit is already contained within its seed. All we need to do is identify the seed for the fruit we wish to harvest. Once we plant and nurture that seed, it will grow and yield its specific fruit. The DNA of that fruit—its greatness, its abundance – is already encoded within the seed.

In the same way, the greatness of the life you were born to live is already within you, contained in your very DNA. Now, we are ready to decode it. Yes, we are ready to unlock it. So, what is that life? What is that dream? What do you truly desire? Take your time. Breathe in deeply and centre yourself. If you haven't found it yet, remain in this state of relaxation and visualisation. Write down everything you see. Visualise where you see yourself, what you do, and how you feel.

What emotions arise from living that life? What fulfilment do you gain from it? Picture the fruits. See them. Savour them. Enjoy the fruits of your greatness. Envision them. Half the journey is complete once you have set your sights on what you desire. This marks the end of today's visualisation session.

As we look ahead to tomorrow, we will take the next step: finding the seeds. The seeds we yearn for that will bear these desired fruits are sourced and chosen with intention. Write down the life you envision. This is your path. This is your authentic identity.

It is your greatness – encoded within you. Write it all down. You are destined for greatness. You are a warrior. You are a victor. You are an overcomer. You are far more powerful than you could ever think or imagine.

Now, wake up with strength, vitality, and the breath of life. Breathe in deeply, relax, and embrace the life you desire. As we move forward to seek the seeds of greatness, know that the whole life you dream of is already within you.

Day two has been designed to help you imagine and visualise your greatness without limits. You are not confined by gender, race, tradition, family background, neighbourhood, or what others may have said about you—whether teachers, parents, or society.

You are being transformed through the renewal of your mind as you visualise the future you desire and deserve. The future you were born to live. This is your birthright. Write down every aspect of the life you long to create and deserve.

You've been reading from Doctor Sylvia Forchap Likambi, a transformational coach and a leading authority on empowerment and transformation in unlocking human potential. Thank you for joining me on this extraordinary journey to unlocking your greatness. May you have a glorious and fulfilling day as you enter this transformational process. Remember, every challenge in life is a tool to shape, refine, and unveil your greatness. Until day three, I wish you an amazing, splendid, and glorious day.

DAY THREE

Unveiling Your Unique Vision

*"The only thing worse than being blind
is having sight but no vision."*
– Helen Keller

"Your vision is the fingerprint of your soul—unique, unparalleled, and meant to leave an indelible mark on the world. Unveil it with courage, nurture it with passion, and watch it transform your reality."

Welcome to day three of your transformational journey to unlocking your greatness with Doctor Sylvia Forchap Likambi. How are you feeling today? I'm thrilled to step further into this journey with you as we embark on the third day of unlocking the greatness that lies within you.

Because you are truly great.

You were born great.
Your greatness is already within you – waiting to be unveiled, unlocked, and released.

Are you ready to continue this incredible transformational journey? Over the next five days, you will unlock your greatness and begin to live the life you were born to: an excellent, glorious, powerful, and exceptional life.

On day two, we visualised the ideal life you desire—free from limitations and barriers. We imagined the perfect seed you would like to sow, unhindered by societal expectations or external constraints.

Now, I want us to shift our focus. Let us transition from visualising in the mind's eye to experiencing something more tangible—something you can see, touch, and feel in your physical reality.

On day two, you were seeing with your spiritual eyes. You were guided by your heart. If you saw that picture, that life, if you desired it so profoundly, it is because you were created to live it. Remember, that seed of greatness, that yearning, was deposited within you by your Creator—placed there at the moment of your conception by your Heavenly Father.

As we step into day three, we will explore this life further. Let's imagine it in more detail. Let's visualise a tangible reality, a clearer picture of the fruits stemming from your greatness's seeds.

Looking at a seed doesn't immediately reveal the full beauty or nature of the fruit it will produce. Yet, within that seed lies every detail of the fruits to come. Similarly, the seeds of your greatness promise an abundant and extraordinary life.

Now, I want you to shift your focus to a beautiful garden. Picture it vividly. Let your mind settle into a calm and relaxed state. Breathe in deeply. You know how to enter this relaxed state—just as we practised on day two.

Relax your shoulders.
Drop them gently.
Feel your shoulder muscles release their tension.

Allow every part of your body to soften, from the top of your head to the soles of your feet. Relax your head, your facial muscles, and your ears. Let go of all tightness.

Let your neck relax. Release those muscles—don't stiffen them. Sit back or lie down, whichever feels most comfortable. Let your entire being become still and at ease, as you did yesterday.

Now, focus on relaxing your arms. Let your elbows, hands, and fingers feel loose and weightless. Drop everything. Let your head gently move from side to side—slowly, smoothly. Rotate it forward and backwards, feeling the tension melt away.

Let your body soften even further. Relax your stomach. Please don't hold it in or tense it. Let those muscles rest, free from contraction.

Relax your legs, your knees, your toes. Let the soles of your feet soften completely. Whether sitting upright or lying on your bed, surrender to deep breathing. Let go of all your thoughts and worries.

Remember, every worry has been taken away. The wind has swept away every challenge, trial, limitation, and obstacle—the same wind you felt on that beach. On day two, that wind carried away the burdens of your past and brought you a new life overflowing with abundance, filled with everything you've ever hoped for or desired.

Now, you are free of limitations. Breathe deeply, feel the air enter your nostrils and fill your lungs. Hold it for a moment, then exhale in total surrender, releasing everything as you relax.

Breathe in again—slow and deep. Hold it, and then let it go. Be completely at ease. I want you to imagine yourself sitting in a beautiful garden. This is your garden—a sacred space gifted to you as part of this transformational journey towards unlocking your greatness.

Picture yourself sitting at the very centre of this garden. It's stunning, peaceful, and vast—the most beautiful garden you could ever imagine.

But for now, the garden is bare. Nothing has been planted yet. It is untouched, yet its soil is incredibly fertile, brimming with potential. This garden can produce the most exquisite flowers, the most luscious fruits, the most vibrant grass, and the tallest, most majestic trees.

The soil is rich and receptive, ready to bring forth life. The garden stretches endlessly, beyond the limits of your physical sight. Its vastness is awe-inspiring.

And here you are, in the middle of this magnificent space, entrusted with its care. This is your garden—virgin soil, pure and untouched. You are its owner, its master, its custodian. You have been given full authority over this space. You alone will decide what to plant, how to nurture it, and what fruits you wish to reap.

The wind stirs gently around you, reminding you of the promise of growth and possibility. This is your moment. You've been gifted this garden. What will you do with it?

What fruits do you want to grow here? What vision do you have for this garden? Take a moment to picture it.

Imagine the fruits you want to harvest. See them as if they're already growing—tangible, vibrant, and alive. Envision the oranges, mangoes, tangerines, grapefruits, or grapes that fill this garden. Perhaps you see colourful flowers or fragrant herbs alongside them. Whatever you desire, picture it vividly.

This is the season of harvest. Your role is to select the fruits with the seeds that will yield the fruits you envision. Every manufacturer starts with the end product in mind, working backwards to create it. Likewise, you are creating the garden of your dreams.

See the result now—the fruits, the flowers, the herbs, and every other product you desire to harvest. Feel them, touch them, and know they are yours to re-create and enjoy. This garden is your canvas, and the fruits it will yield are yours to define.

Before you were even conceived, before you were formed in your mother's womb, your destiny had already been envisaged. It was encoded within the DNA found in your mother's egg and your father's sperm, destined to fuse and give birth to the extraordinary person you were always meant to become. Your greatness was not an accident; it was carefully envisioned, wrapped, and placed within you as a seed of greatness waiting to be nurtured and unleashed into the world.

So, as we look at the fruits you want to grow, ask yourself: What do you want to plant? What do you wish to sow in the garden of your life? Remember, this garden is yours alone. It is not for your neighbour or anyone else to plant in. This garden is sacred, entrusted to you to cultivate and produce fruits that will benefit you and nourish your children, your children's children, and generations to come. These fruits will bring you fulfilment, satisfaction, and joy.

Now, visualise those fruits. Imagine yourself harvesting them. See yourself gathering ripe, beautiful oranges full of colour and vitality. Picture yourself collecting and bringing them into your home, laying them out in your kitchen or living room. Imagine peeling the oranges, their sweet fragrance filling the air, and savouring the first bite of their juicy, refreshing flesh.

Even though you planted a single orange seed, you're now reaping an abundant harvest. One seed has produced an entire tree laden with oranges—not just enough for you but plenty to share. Envision yourself again peeling the oranges, squeezing out their juice, and relishing every sip. Perhaps it's a hot summer day, and that chilled, freshly squeezed juice refreshes and revives you. Your thirst is quenched, and you feel restored and energised.

This imagery isn't just about the fruit itself—it's a metaphor for your greatness. The fruits you harvest represent the culmination of your potential, the final product of the greatness always within you. That seed of greatness is ready to be unlocked, sown, nurtured, and grown into something extraordinary for the world to see and appreciate.

But ask yourself: Why do you desire these fruits in your garden and not others? For example, why oranges and not guavas? Why mangoes and not lemons? Why grapes and not passionfruit? Why apples and not bananas?

Your choices matter. The fruits you choose to cultivate reflect your desires, your purpose, and the vision you hold for your life. What is driving your choices? What is the force behind your decisions?

Your "why" is crucial. It's the motive that fuels your actions. It's the force that will keep you going, sowing, toiling, and nurturing your garden, even when challenges arise or you feel like giving up. Your "why" will push you forward when motivation diminishes and will ignite your will to keep going when the journey feels difficult.

So, establish your "why" right now. Why do you want these fruits? What is the deeper meaning behind your choices? Perhaps it's your satisfaction when you see the oranges you've worked so hard to grow. Maybe it's the joy of sharing your harvest with loved ones or the fulfilment of knowing your efforts have borne fruit—literally and figuratively.

Your "why" is the driving force that will propel you towards unlocking your greatness. Hold onto it. Let it guide and sustain you as you embark on this transformational journey.

Perhaps there is a profound sense of quenching your thirst when you picture yourself consuming these oranges. A sense of fulfilment. A sense of refreshment. Revival. Satisfaction. Is that what you feel? Is that the reason you desire these fruits? Or is it because your neighbour has those same fruits? Think about it carefully. The latter is not a strong enough motive. If your desire is based on someone else's choices—on what your neighbour has—what will happen when your neighbour no longer values those fruits? What will happen if they no longer bring satisfaction to them? Will you stop desiring them, too?

Your motives must be rooted in something bigger and more profound. They cannot depend on your neighbours', spouses', parents', siblings', or friends'. No! Those motives will fail you when challenges arise. They won't be strong enough to push you forward when you feel like giving up.

Your "why" must come from within. It must focus on revival, refreshment, satisfaction, and a sense of accomplishment—peace, rest, and fulfilment. It must evoke that "aha!" moment, the feeling of, *Yes! This is what I've been searching for my whole life. This is it.* It should resonate deeply within you, sparking joy and alignment with your authentic self.

Imagine the fruit you've desired since you were born. Picture how it tastes—so good, so sweet. You know the impact it has on your health, your well-being, and your energy. Feel it. Engage all your senses in this vision of fulfilment and satisfaction. Because that is why you were given this desire—it's a part of your greatness.

If your desire doesn't produce these feelings of satisfaction, rest, accomplishment, and fulfilment, then it may not be the greatness that was divinely placed within you. Instead, it might stem from what society deems necessary or the expectations of your parents, siblings, or spouse. It could be shaped by the limitations others have placed on you—by how far they told you that you could go or how far you've allowed yourself to see.

Remember, you can only go as far as you can see. That's why, at the beginning of this journey, I took you beyond limitations, obstacles and challenges into a state of boundless freedom—a place where you could dream without barriers.

So now, what fruits are you going to harvest? What seeds will you plant in your garden? These choices must be based on satisfaction and fulfilment, that deep sense of *wow!* What life do you desire?

What can you see yourself doing that brings you complete rest and joy and finally makes you feel settled?

When you find that fruit and know what it is, congratulations! I'm so proud of you. This is your defining moment. This is the turning point—from seed to fruit, from soil to harvest, from imagination and idea to reality and realisation.

Welcome to your greatness. Welcome to the life you were born to live. Welcome to your birthright, authentic self, and life's purpose—which brings immense fulfilment, joy, and a divine sense of settlement.

Now that you have seen the fruits and understand why—you can see, feel, and experience it—you yearn to harvest that fruit. Let's go! Let's go and gather those fruits. You have them in your hands now. Let's open them up. You don't need to look any further to find the seeds, for they are already within the fruits you've harvested. These seeds are the key to your greatness.

What you see is what you can achieve. Because you see greatness, you can touch it because it's a tangible reality, manifesting in the physical. It's right here in your hands. You're holding it—the life you've desired, the fruit you've longed for.

Now, break open that fruit and collect the seeds. You are certain of the seeds within it. There's no mistake, no room for error. You can't confuse an orange seed for a lemon seed simply because of the people around you, your neighbours, or the circles you belong to. Similarly, your identity isn't determined by those you associate with, your social class, or your environment. That's why it's essential to find *your* seeds—extract them directly from your source—within, these represent your authentic self.

When conceived, your DNA already contained everything you were destined to become. Now, we are unlocking that DNA, decoding the essence of your greatness. Your DNA is unique—there's only one version on this planet. Even identical twins don't share the same DNA. You don't have the same DNA as your parents, either. This is your blueprint, your unmistakable identity, your authentic greatness.

Let's work from your DNA, the blueprint that defines who you are. There's no exchange, no substitution. It's your identity. Let's begin decoding it—unlocking the potential that has always been within you.

The codes of your greatness are ready to be revealed, step by step, bringing to life the incredible individual you were born to be.

Imagine holding that orange in your hands now. See yourself in your kitchen or living room, breaking it open. The excitement is overwhelming! You know why you want this fruit, you understand its value, and you can feel how refreshing and fulfilling it is. Remember, when an orange seed is sown, it doesn't produce just one orange—it grows into a tree that bears countless oranges. That is the power of what's within you: the seed of greatness, the potential for abundance, and the capacity to nurture and share the fruits of your labour with the world.

When there is abundance, people come to harvest, and more can benefit. That's perfectly fine—it's okay. So, take the seed of that amazing fruit you desire to see in your garden. Not the fruit your neighbour desires or your mother, siblings, or children want—the fruit *you* desire.

You'll naturally want to share when you achieve a good harvest and experience true joy. Your happiness will overflow, and you'll want to invite your neighbours, friends, and guests into your home. You'll say, "Come and take some! I've got an abundant harvest and plenty of oranges. If I don't share them, they'll go to waste." You'll find fulfilment in announcing your harvest and welcoming others to partake in it.

When it's your harvest, the fruits you truly love, the excitement will compel you to tell your friends and neighbours. You'll want to describe the fruits vividly, sharing their amazing benefits. You'll inspire them with your passion and transformation as they witness the positive effects the fruits have had on you. From eating the fruits of your labour, you'll exude vitality, energy, and health—your glowing complexion and well-being will be unmistakable.

This is why others will be inspired by you and drawn to join you in your feast. They'll celebrate with you because your greatness isn't meant for you alone—it's too vast to be contained. It is greatness, beyond what eyes have seen, or ears have heard, and it's meant to be shared with the world.

So now, with the fruits in your hands, you've also taken their seeds. Remember, you cannot desire oranges unless you've held them, seen them, and know how they taste and their benefits. Knowledge is key. This means no one can bring you an apple and convince you it's an orange. You recognise the fruit by its characteristics. Even if you don't know what an apple seed looks like, you know the apple itself—enough to avoid confusion.

Similarly, you cannot desire grapes, yet, settle for oranges, or seek mangoes and end up with passionfruit. You won't find a mango seed inside when you break open a passionfruit. You'll only find seeds that will produce more passionfruit. The fruit you hold determines the seeds you'll plant.

Come with me—hold the fruit in your hands once again. Smell it, see it, taste it, study it. I love mangoes, for instance. I recognise their colour, the ease with which the peel comes off when they're ripe, the succulent juiciness, and the sweetness that bursts forth when I eat them. I savour the pleasure and satisfaction they bring, filling me until I'm gratified.

Now, get your fruit. Be certain it's the one you desire. Take out its seeds. Congratulations—you're holding the seeds of your greatness. You can be confident these are the right seeds, carrying the key to unlocking your true potential.

The seeds hold the unique DNA of your greatness, the codes that define your purpose. All we need to do now is decode them, unlock the door and step into the life we were meant to live. This is where knowledge becomes a powerful tool, but it doesn't stop there. The application of knowledge—*wisdom*—is where transformation begins.

These seeds hold the potential to grow and reproduce the greatness already within you. Here's the beautiful truth: you don't need to search far and wide for greatness. You don't need to travel to distant lands or look for external sources to find what you need to sow and cultivate the life you were born to live. Everything you need is already in your hands, encoded in your DNA, waiting to be unlocked.

Like the orange seed that carries within it the promise of countless oranges, your greatness is inherent, awaiting the right conditions to flourish. Sowing these seeds is akin to decoding the unique greatness within you. This process—the nurturing, growing, and eventual flourishing—leads to the magnificent fruits of your labour. The effort, time, and care you invest in nurturing your greatness will yield an abundant harvest.

Hence, holding the fruit and never opening or tasting it is insufficient. Without opening and tasting it, how can you truly know its worth? You must take action. With the key in hand, you must open the door. After all, what use is holding the key to your own home if you never use it?

If you don't take action, if you don't reach for the door, place the key into the keyhole, and turn it, the door will never be unlocked. That door will never open, allowing you to step into that amazing house, extraordinary future, and great individual you've envisaged and were born to become. Action is essential. The application of knowledge holds power and brings about real transformation.

It's time to act—to take those keys, open the door, and walk through with purpose and dignity. The homeowner does not enter through the window; they hold the keys, open the door, and walk freely and majestically into their home whenever they wish, as often as they desire. That's freedom. They don't need permission from anyone to step into their home.

Similarly, *you* don't need anyone's permission to embrace your greatness. You don't need approval from your spouse, parents, siblings, teachers, or neighbours. You don't need to apologise or say, "I'm sorry, I need to open my door now." It's your home, your life, your greatness. So, let's walk into your greatness now! Let's step into the power that resides within you.

Now that you have the seed, we're moving into day four: preparing your garden. You've got the seed and held the fruit in your hands—you've seen, touched, and experienced it. You have your garden, a fertile space ready for cultivation. It's time to start sowing.

But first comes preparation. Preparation is the ultimate act of faith in the unseen. Imagine yourself in that beautiful garden, still in the middle. You've seen the fruits you desire; you understand why you desire them. You've even taken part in the harvest, tasted the sweetness, and felt what it's like to live that fulfilled life.

Now, it's time to prepare your garden. Your garden is your mind. As we step into day four, we'll enter a preparation period for sowing. Sowing doesn't happen immediately. First, you till the ground. You prepare that fertile soil. The preparation depends on the type of fruits you want to harvest and the seeds you hold. Some seeds require deeper digging, while others need shallow ridges. Each seed has unique requirements.

On day four, we will step into your mind—your garden—and prepare it for the season of sowing. This preparation ensures that your mind is ready to receive, nurture, and bring forth the seed of greatness within you. That greatness is entwined with your beliefs, waiting to be unlocked.

Thank you for being here. Remember, you are great, a victor, and destined for greatness. You were born to thrive and soar to greater heights. Every challenge you face in life carries a profound message for you to learn and grow from.

What you see now as a stumbling block is, in fact, a stepping stone, lifting you to greater altitudes. Picture that orange hanging on the tree. What you perceive as an obstacle is the ladder that brings you closer to the fruit. It's a platform that allows you to stretch out, grasp the orange, and reap the rewards of what you've sown.

This is your moment. This is your time!

DAY FOUR

Unlock the Transformational Power of Your Mind

"*Do not conform to the pattern of this world, but be transformed by the renewing of your mind. Then you will be able to test and approve what God's will is—his good, pleasing and perfect will.*"
-Romans 12:2

Welcome to Day Four of your transformational journey to unlocking your greatness with Dr Sylvia Forchap-Likambi. It's a privilege to join you again on this inspiring path to unlocking the greatness within you. Today, we build upon the powerful foundations laid in the previous days, moving ever closer to realising the greatness within you.

On day three, you held the vision of your greatness as tangible fruits—a clear, concrete manifestation of your dreams and purpose.

This followed the work of day two when you envisioned the ideal life you desired and deserved. By day three, your greatness became more than an idea; it was something you could touch, see, and hold in your hands—a manifestation of the fruits you desire: peace, joy, love, patience, kindness, and more.

On day four, we venture into the metaphorical garden of your life—a vast, boundless terrain awaiting cultivation. This garden represents the limitless potential within you, an infinite space without boundaries or limitations. Your garden is your mind, infinite and stretching as far as your imagination and determination can take it. Nevertheless, the potential of your garden lies dormant until you take deliberate action.

Today, on Day Four, we step into the powerful realm of your mind—your garden—and the vital process of conserving your seed of greatness. This is where we ensure that the seed is neither neglected nor aborted before it has the chance to grow. Like soil cradling a seed, your mind must nurture and sustain your potential through every stage of its journey—from taking root and the first sprout to a gigantic tree bearing abundant fruit. Even when the tree matures, the soil remains essential, anchoring its roots and providing continuous nourishment until it bears fruit that others can enjoy.

When you are joyful, those around you naturally benefit from the overflow of your joy. Your peace radiates outward, creating an atmosphere of serenity for those in your presence. Just as a tree drops ripe mangoes, your fruits—peace, joy, love—become gifts to those who encounter you. Your light shines effortlessly, guiding and uplifting others, often without you even realising it.

However, for this to happen, your mind must be a prepared and receptive ground. A seed left in a cupboard, no matter how potent, will remain a seed forever. Without planting and nurturing, it cannot grow into a tree or bear fruit. Likewise, your greatness—though encoded within you—requires action. You must sow, nurture, and nourish your potential to unlock the power within you.

Your mind is the gateway, the bridge between your spirit—where the seed of greatness resides—and the visible fruits in your life. Your spirit holds the seed, unseen yet full of potential, and the fruits it produces become the evidence of your growth. The gap between the life you envision and the life you experience is measured by time—and by the actions you take to bridge that gap.

The sooner you sow the seeds of greatness and begin to nurture them, the closer you are to realising your vision. Taking action shortens the time between planting and harvest. Missing a season delays the harvest, so you must seize every moment to sow, nurture, and act. Your commitment to preparing your mind and cultivating your potential will determine the abundance of your harvest.

Your mind is a powerful tool, the key that connects your spirit to the fruits of your greatness. By aligning your thoughts, beliefs, and actions, you create the fertile soil needed for your dreams to take root and flourish. From this foundation, your vision transforms into reality, and your greatness unfolds—not just for your benefit, but for the world around you.

Imagine for a moment what would happen if you chose not to sow the seeds from your fruit. The cycle would end if you consumed the fruit without planting its seeds. The same is true for your greatness. If you fail to nurture and develop your potential and gifts—your greatness will remain entrapped and futile. Greatness is not just about personal success. It is about leaving a legacy—creating a meaningful and transformational experience that endures long after we are gone. When you sow the seeds of your greatness in others, you ensure that your impact extends beyond your lifetime.

Think of the young generation. If we consume the fruits of our labour without planting new seeds, we risk depriving future generations of the wisdom, knowledge, and inspiration they need to thrive. By mentoring, teaching, and empowering others, we pass on the legacy of greatness.

When you decide not to develop and reproduce yourself, not to mentor or empower others, not to bless the world with your gifts, you risk allowing your greatness to fade away. If you do not sow those seeds into others—the young, the youth, children, or the community—you fail to replenish the world with your unique attributes and greatness. And what happens then? It ends with you. Your footprint is absent when you depart this earth, leaving no trace of the extraordinary gifts you were given to share with the world.

What a shame future generation would miss out because we chose only to enjoy the fruits but neglected to sow the seeds. Imagine the potential lost when we don't mentor, nurture, or empower others to become as great—or even greater—than ourselves.

Imagine standing before a tree loaded with fruit. The fruit is your vision, your greatness, your purpose. Imagine sharing that fruit with others, planting its seeds in the fertile soil of their minds and hearts. This is how you create a ripple effect, transforming not just your life but the lives of countless others.

I use metaphors and analogies to help you connect with this journey. Think of yourself as a great tree, deeply rooted and nourished by the soil from which you draw strength and sustenance. At the start of this journey, we spoke about the power of knowledge and the even more remarkable power of wisdom—the application of that knowledge. Now, let's consider the seeds within your fruits. These seeds represent your beliefs.

While you are not a tree, the analogy helps illuminate a profound truth: your beliefs, like seeds, can shape your reality. Your desired fruit is already in your hand; you know its shape, colour, and texture. You know how it tastes and the satisfaction it brings. Similarly, you can see your vision, feel its power, and sense the fulfilment that living in alignment with your purpose will bring.

Your beliefs are the seeds from which greatness grows. Without these seeds, there can be no fruit. Without these beliefs, there can be no reproduction or replenishment of the greatness you desire and envisage.

On this fourth day, I invite you to focus on your mind and the beliefs you hold about yourself. Do you believe in the seeds of greatness within you? Do you believe you can nurture and grow them to create a life of abundance, purpose, and fulfilment? Remember, everything you need is already within you—ready to be cultivated and nurtured into the fruits of your greatness. Stay rooted in this truth as we continue this transformational journey together.

Let us now return to the metaphor of the garden—your mind—where the seeds of your greatness will be sown. As a gardener tills the soil, removing weeds and ensuring fertile ground, you must prepare your mind to receive and nurture the seeds of greatness. This preparation involves clearing doubts, fears, and limiting beliefs that may hinder your growth. Only then will you be able to sow seeds of greatness that can grow into your desired life. It requires self-belief and faith—a deep trust in the unseen potential within you.

Preparation is the greatest evidence of faith—things hoped for but not yet visible. Preparing your mind creates a grounded and fertile environment for your beliefs to take root and flourish. Your preparation may differ depending on the type of fruit you want to harvest. Some seeds require deep digging, while others thrive in shallow soil. The key is to know your vision and understand what is needed to bring it to life.

Cultivating A Growth Mindset

"We can't become what we need to be by remaining what we are."
—Oprah Winfrey

We must shine a light on your beliefs to sow the seeds of your greatness. As previously stated, your beliefs are like seeds—hidden from view yet fundamental to your growth. No one can see your beliefs; they are deeply embedded within you, shaping your values, thoughts, words, actions, habits, and destiny.

Furthermore, your beliefs shape how you perceive life, yourself, your past, and your future. They define your sense of greatness and power. Though unseen, they influence every facet of your being, guiding your decisions and priorities. "Truly I tell you, whoever says to this mountain, Be lifted and thrown into the sea! He does not doubt in his heart but believes that what he says will take place; it will be done for him." *Mark 11:23*

Your beliefs, thoughts, and values are deeply personal, yet, they are part of the unique blueprint encoded in your DNA. As already mentioned and highlighted several times in the book, before you were born and even conceived, the Almighty God had already established the incredible individual you are destined to become. Your greatness was set in motion, and the seeds of belief were planted within you—to believe in your greatness and manifest it in due season.

Yet, the beauty and challenges of humanity lie in free will. You are not obliged to hold on to these beliefs destined to shape your destiny. You have the power to choose what you believe and what you reject. This makes your beliefs uniquely yours, defining your values, shaping your thoughts, and ultimately influencing who you become—in alignment with your greatness and divine purpose or contrary to the latter. This is because your thoughts, formed from your beliefs, shape your words. If you are optimistic, you indeed speak optimism. You talk about life and positivity, creating an atmosphere that reflects these qualities. Your words (spoken or written), in turn, inspire your actions.

For example, when you write down your vision and set definite goals to accomplish it, those written words transform into deliberate actions. Words, initially born as thoughts, become tangible realities through action. Goals rooted in your values and beliefs guide your life, shaping your habits and destiny.

Your inherent belief in your vision, fruits, and greatness inspires you to take the necessary actions to bring them to fruition. You sow the seeds, nurture your potential, and commit to cultivating a growth mindset—one that prepares the soil—your mind—to receive and nurture your greatness. You also refuse to let self-doubt, negativity, or limiting beliefs hold you back.

With a belief system rooted in positivity and purpose, you create the conditions for growth. You prepare the ground to plant the seeds and tend them diligently, allowing your greatness to flourish and leave a lasting legacy for generations. Hence, preparing the soil is vital. Preparation is a critical step in the journey of transformation.

Understand that your beliefs, thoughts, and actions are the keys to unlocking your greatness. Your beliefs are the invisible foundation of this process. As previously highlighted, no one can see what you believe, but your beliefs shape your values—your core principles and convictions about life, success, and your purpose. These values, in turn, influence your thoughts, shaping how you perceive yourself, the world around you, and who you become. As you may know, "As a man thinks, so he is."

The soil of your mind is where your beliefs take root. The quality of this soil determines the strength and health of your beliefs. Just like a plant requires good soil to grow strong and healthy, your beliefs require a fertile and nurturing mind to thrive. If your mind is rigid, unreceptive, or full of doubts and negativity, the roots of your beliefs (seeds of greatness) won't take hold, and your potential will remain trapped and untapped.

When preparing your garden, you must be mindful of any hindrances in the soil that could prevent your seeds from taking root. You cannot plant your seeds there if rocks are in the way. Similarly, in your mind, unresolved issues or negative thought patterns will prevent your beliefs from taking root.

To ensure your greatness is not hindered, you must identify and remove any obstacles in your mind. These obstacles may be negative self-talk, past failures, or limiting beliefs ingrained in you over time. By identifying and removing these obstacles, you create space for your beliefs to grow and your potential to be realised.

Weeding Out Negativity

> *"Weeding out the harmful influences should become the norm not the exception."* –Carlos Wallace

Weeds in a garden can quickly overtake the plants you've worked so hard to grow. Similarly, negative thoughts and influences can quickly take over your mind if you don't tend to them. It's essential to be vigilant and remove these weeds as soon as they appear. Just as a gardener regularly inspects their garden for weeds, you must regularly check in with your thoughts and beliefs. If negativity or doubt creeps in, "pull it out immediately" and replace it with positive thoughts and faith.

The key to weeding out negativity is awareness. When you become aware of your thoughts, you can immediately address them. If a thought arises that doesn't align with your greatness, challenge it—replace it with a thought that reinforces your belief in your potential. Over time, as you continue to "pull out" and ultimately disregard the weeds of doubt and fear—replacing them with confidence and faith, your garden will flourish, and your greatness will shine through.

Your words, whether spoken, written, or decreed, are not just expressions of thought. They are seeds of action. Once you articulate your goals and vision, you give them life. Written goals, spoken affirmations, and declared intentions transform into actions—the tangible steps you must take toward realising your dreams and greatness.

Actions repeated consistently over time form habits. Research shows that habits develop in as little as 21 to 28 days. When your actions become habitual, they no longer feel like effort; they become second nature, seamlessly integrated into your life. This is how you build momentum and prepare your mind to be receptive, moving closer and closer to the greatness you envision.

As we end this chapter, I urge you to invest in your mind and develop a growth mindset. Clear away any obstacles or doubts. Nurture your mind with faith, determination, and purpose.

This is your journey, your transformation, your time to shine. Your greatness is not just a possibility but a reality waiting to be unlocked. Let us continue forward together as we prepare to sow the seeds of your greatness and step into the life you were born to live.

DAY FIVE

Affirming Your Greatness: Awakening the Power Within

"I came to the conclusion that there is an existential moment in your life when you must decide to speak for yourself; nobody else can speak for you."
– Martin Luther King Jr.

Welcome to Day Five of your transformational journey to unlocking your greatness with Dr. Sylvia Forchap Likambi. It is a privilege and an honour to accompany you on this remarkable journey of self-discovery and transformation. By reaching this pivotal moment in your journey, you have already demonstrated a level of commitment and resilience that is truly inspiring. You are on your way to realising the incredible potential that lies within you. Congratulations on reaching this milestone. You are a victor, embodying greatness, for the seed of greatness resides within you.

On Day Four, we ventured into the metaphorical garden of your life – your mind, a vast, boundless expanse full of possibilities waiting to be cultivated. Today, on Day Five, we continue on the foundations laid down on Day Four by focusing on preparing the soil of your mind, ensuring it is fertile enough to receive and cultivate the seeds of greatness, allowing it to thrive and flourish. Your mind grants access and provides the foundation for growth. It is a powerful tool, the gateway to transformation. It is the soil through which the spiritual seed of greatness in you will grow and bear fruit. Yet, if negativity, fear, or doubt hardens your soil, the seed cannot thrive. Rocks of pessimism, cemented by limiting beliefs and societal conditioning, can suffocate your potential.

Negativity is toxic. It hardens the mind, making it resistant to change and growth. It transforms fertile soil into infertile and hardened soil, preventing seeds from sprouting. Therefore, we must replace negativity with optimism, faith, and affirmations.

If your garden has been cemented, you cannot expect the seed sown beneath to grow. It cannot break through; it tries, pushing with all its might, but it is trapped.

This is why we often struggle to break free from the boundaries and restrictions society imposes—the labels and the boxes we fit into—but we fail. We have been confined and cemented, and our greatness lies buried beneath the surface, striving to push through but unable to break free. It is stifled and held down.

Imagine the sorrow of a world filled with orange seeds that never grew to bear fruit or a great man whose potential was evident, yet his greatness was never realised. His brilliance remained hidden, never manifesting.

For your seed of greatness to thrive and flourish, your mind must be receptive, open, and fertile. This requires breaking free from societal labels and limitations, clearing the mental debris of negativity, self-doubt, and fear, and overcoming limiting beliefs. You cannot allow your mind to become barren. Instead, you must cultivate it for growth, creating an environment where positivity and possibility flourish.

Your mind must be ready and receptive, even if your circumstances have conditioned you otherwise. Perhaps your upbringing, financial situation, environment, or society have moulded your mind in a way that hinders its receptiveness to greatness. Now is the time to recondition it. Make your mind fertile ground, free of negativity and ready to nurture the seed of your potential.

Affirmations are powerful tools we can use to recondition the mind. They are declarations of belief, spoken aloud, that shape our reality. By affirming the qualities and life we desire, we speak greatness into existence. Words have power—to build, create, and transform.

Affirmations help us recondition the mind, creating fertile soil for growth—they are similar to fertilisers that speed up the growth process. They replace limiting beliefs with empowering ones. By repeatedly affirming our greatness, we train our minds to expect it, bringing us closer to manifesting it.

This process mirrors the placebo effect: when you believe in something, even something as simple as water, it can bring healing. Similarly, when you proclaim greatness, even if it isn't your current reality, you attract the resources, people, and opportunities needed to manifest it. When you believe in your affirmations, your actions align with them, and the universe responds. Opportunities, resources, and people gravitate toward you, guiding you toward your vision.

Your mind is like a sponge, absorbing whatever you expose it to. Fill it with positivity, light, and possibility. As you prepare your mind, envision the greatness within you, waiting to emerge. See yourself as the person you desire to become, living the life you yearn for.

Speak boldly about your future. Call forth the greatness within you as though it already exists. Imagine yourself achieving your goals and fulfilling your potential. Your words shape your reality. They nurture the seeds of greatness in the fertile soil of your mind. By continuously affirming your potential, you create the conditions for growth and transformation.

Avoid focusing on the negatives or what you do not want. Instead, direct your energy toward what you want. We must replace negativity with positivity. If you focus on what you don't want—on the things you wish to avoid—you unintentionally affirm them. For example, instead of saying, "I don't want negativity in my life," consider positively framing your affirmation: "I love positivity, and positive people surround me." Remember, your words shape your reality, so it's important to frame your desires in a way that assumes they are already happening.

In this journey, we will replace limiting beliefs and negative thought patterns with positive, empowering affirmations. Frame your desires in the present tense like they are already a reality.

Write down your affirmations. Frame them. Place them where you can see them and repeat them often. Speak them with conviction. For instance:

- "I am great."
- "I am a creator, made in the image of the Almighty God."
- "I am light to the world, and my light shines brightly."
- "I am joy, peace, and kindness."
- "I am successful, living the life of abundance designed for me."
- "I am a symbol of greatness, leaving a lasting legacy."

- "I am a multimillionaire, living in abundance and sharing my wealth to change the world."
- "I am a transformational speaker, inspiring and empowering others."
- "I am a beacon of light, bringing light, joy, and peace to those around me."

Besides being fertiliser, these affirmations also act as the water and nutrients that nourish the seeds of greatness you are planting. They will enrich the soil of your mind and create the ideal conditions for growth. Here are a few more affirmations for you:

- "I am greatness personified."
- "I am worthy of success, joy, and love."
- "I am aligned with my purpose."
- "My life is abundant, and I am grateful for it."
- "Every day, in every way, I am becoming a better version of myself."
- "I am a unique and valuable individual."
- "I embrace my flaws and turn them into strengths."
- "I am confident in my abilities and trust in my journey."
- "I honour my purpose and step boldly into my future and greatness."

Speak these affirmations with conviction, as though they are already your reality. The more you say them, the more you begin to believe them. Your words can reshape your beliefs and mindset, creating your life's external circumstances. As a farmer who nurtures crops with water and fertiliser to ensure growth, you must nurture your seeds of greatness with empowering affirmations.

Affirmations are one of the most direct ways to consciously align your energy with the life you want to create. By repeating these affirmations daily, you are reprogramming your mind, creating new neuronal pathways, and sending a powerful signal to the universe that you are ready to receive all you desire. Remember, thoughts become things, and words become actions. What you think and say is what you will ultimately create.

The power of affirmations also lies in their connection to the Law of Attraction. This universal law states that like attracts like and that the energy we emit into the world is the energy that will come back to us. The more you affirm greatness, success, peace, and joy, the more you attract these traits and qualities into your life. Your thoughts and words create a vibrational frequency that aligns with your desires.

As we prepare the soil of your mind, it's important to remember that the greatness you are cultivating is authentic to who you are. Societal norms, labels, or expectations do not define you. You are not a reflection of what others think you should be or your past. Your greatness is unique, and it is time to embrace it fully.

What you focus on shapes your reality. Therefore, filling your mind with thoughts that align with your true essence and authentic self is important. Visualise yourself as the person you aspire to become—imagine the qualities you wish to embody and see yourself living the life you have always dreamed of.

As you continue to affirm your greatness, remember that you are not just speaking words—creating and aligning your authentic self with your actions. The affirmations you speak will align with your heart's desires, designed to make you the best version of yourself.

These affirmations reinforce the greatness within you and help you tap into your authentic power. You are stepping into your true essence, a crucial part of the process. Your mind must accept and internalise that you are destined for greatness.

As we conclude Day Five, your mind is undergoing a renewal. You are ready to sow the seeds of greatness with intention and care. Your mind is fertile and prepared to accept the seeds of peace, joy, and success. Remember, societal labels and expectations do not define you. You can embrace your authentic self and live a life filled with purpose and fulfilment.

Tomorrow, Day Six, we will begin sowing these seeds in earnest. We will explore the seasons of life, the importance of patience, and how to take intentional action to cultivate the life we desire. Each day brings us another step toward your transformation.

Thank you for joining me on this remarkable journey. Together, we are unlocking the greatness within you, one step at a time. Keep affirming your worth, potential, and greatness, and remember that you are already on the path to becoming the person you were always meant to be.

Thank you, and may your mind continue to blossom as you cultivate the greatness within you.

DAY SIX

Anchored in Purpose: Standing Firm in Your Convictions

"Everything you need to rise, to transform, and to thrive is already within you. Awaken your inner power, and step boldly into your destiny."

Welcome to Day Six of your transformational journey towards unlocking your greatness with Dr. Sylvia Forchap Likambi. You are now on day six of your life-changing quest to realise your full potential and step into the greatness you were born to embody. On Day Six, we will explore in depth the infinite potential of your garden—your mind. As discussed in previous chapters, this is the fertile ground where everything will flourish, and where sowing and reaping will occur. Up to this point, we have been preparing the garden and the soil to ensure they are receptive to the seed.

On Day Five, we harnessed the power of positive affirmations to cultivate it. As you know, a seed can only germinate and flourish in a fertile environment. It cannot grow in rocky or barren soil. Your mind, too, must be receptive and fertile for the greatness within you to emerge.

Today, we continue to highlight the transformational power and potential of the mind, framed by the metaphor of a kingdom ruled by a queen and governed by stewards and governors. The queen symbolises the divine spirit, while the stewards and governors represent the mind—the pathway through which divine purpose is realised. The mind should be guided by the spirit rather than by the physical, external world. Much like a kingdom where stewards follow the queen's instructions to direct the workers, the mind must adhere to the guidance of your higher purpose, steering clear of the distractions and limitations of the physical realm.

We emphasise the importance of understanding the mind's role in unlocking your greatness. Just as an orange seed focuses on becoming an orange tree, you must focus on becoming your true self without being distracted by external pressures or comparisons to others. The seed metaphor also highlights the concept that everything you need to grow into greatness is already within you. With an open and receptive mind guided by your beliefs, vision, and purpose, you can achieve the greatness you are destined for, regardless of your circumstances.

Understanding the Nature of the Mind and the Power of Belief

I want you to develop a deeper understanding of the nature of the mind and how it functions. Your mind is the gateway through which your seed will grow and transform into the tree, the person you are destined to become and the results you wish to achieve. It is within your mind that the transformation occurs—from seed to tree, from potential to greatness. The mind is where the spiritual and the physical converge. It is where the transaction occurs between the spiritual—eternal, unseen, and intangible — and the physical, the reality we experience.

Your beliefs are spiritual, eternal, and cannot be seen or touched, yet they shape your reality and life experiences. The spiritual realm influences the physical world, not the other way around. This is why the seeds you sow in your mind will determine the harvest you reap. The fruits—the tangible outcomes —come from the seeds planted in the unseen spiritual world of your mind rather than from the physical world itself.

Your daily actions reflect the seeds you have sown in your mind. The spiritual seed determines the type of fruits—or results—you will achieve. The physical realm cannot dominate the spiritual; it is unable to comprehend or measure your beliefs. It is inconceivable that a person born into poverty with illiterate parents who have never attended school could dream of becoming the President of the United States. The physical world—the circumstances, statistics, studies, and polls—can never grasp such a dream. This is precisely what Barack Obama accomplished, although this is not to suggest that his parents were illiterate.

The world could not comprehend how a young African-American from humble beginnings could have the audacity to believe he could become the president of the United States. Every piece of research, every statistic, pointed to the opposite outcome. However, none of these physical forces could determine the final result. Barack Obama's success was not a consequence of the physical world's understanding but rather his unshakeable belief in himself. His belief was the foundation that shaped and defined who he would become.

And so it is for you. Against all odds, whether people like you or not, whether they respect your background, gender, religion, skin colour, or appearance, is irrelevant. Your beliefs will find a way to emerge from your mind and become the words you speak with conviction. And words, as we know, are powerful—they can either give life or cause death. You will speak life into every aspect of your life—your career, your relationships, your dreams. This is the power of belief, and it is your belief that shapes your reality.

You must never let your condition define who you are or will become. The physical world—your present and current circumstances—cannot represent you. Your beliefs, rooted deep within your mind, will determine your path and unlock your true greatness.

The Battlefield of the Mind

Every battle in life takes place in your mind, on the battlefield of your thoughts. A battlefield is where war, conflict, and struggles occur—the clash between life and death, between remaining seed or becoming the fruit you were always meant to be. It is the war between your true potential and current situation, between your greatness and present circumstances.

This is the battlefield of your mind—a war between the physical and the spiritual, between what you see and what you cannot see. It is a battle between what you can touch, feel, and comprehend with your senses and what you can solely envision with your spiritual eyes—your vision, dreams, and desires. The former is placed within you by a higher power—God, to guide you and sustain your hopes, regardless of your current circumstances.

Even in the face of poverty, your desires and dreams should never fade, for they are the essence of hope. Only the living can hope, and as long as you hold onto hope, your desires will lead you towards your destiny and greatness. They serve as reminders of who you are and your inherent greatness.

The divine placed your desires there as a guide, a force that directs you towards your purpose. You must focus on that spiritual force within you. The physical world can never win over the spiritual. It cannot even compete with the spiritual. Only when you allow external voices to dictate your life, when you listen to others who tell you where you are supposed to be and who you are meant to become, can the physical world suppress your greatness. But rest assured, your greatness is untouchable. Even if it is hidden, it can never be completely gone. The spiritual is not physical, so what is physical cannot affect it.

Your spirit will never yield to the physical body. It is akin to a monarchy, where the king or queen dominates their realm. Just as a mother can nurture and give birth to new life, the spirit has the capacity to foster greatness. Similarly, as the queen governs the kingdom, your spirit governs your life. Your beliefs, like seeds, possess the potential to grow and develop into an extraordinary individual—the person you were always destined to become.

Imagine a kingdom with a queen in control and a prince or princess destined to inherit the throne. The servants in the kingdom do not determine the realm's future. Similarly, your greatness is not dictated by external forces but by your spirit. Your beliefs are the seeds that will shape your destiny.

Within the monarchy, whether we call them the stewards or the governors, these are the figures through whom the king or queen will issue decrees and instructions. These instructions are then conveyed to the servants or workers, who carry out the tasks required. The Queen understands her kingdom's structure, its purpose, and how it must operate to foster great citizens. She passes this information on to the stewards and governors, who, in this metaphor, represent your mind. Your mind is the steward; it is the governor. This aligns with Romans 8:6, which states, 'The mind governed by the flesh is death, but the mind governed by the Spirit is life and peace.'"

You certainly do not want the stewards and governors to receive guidance from the workers and enslaved people in the kingdom. They do not comprehend the kingdom's functionality or the monarchy's origins. The flow of authority must proceed from the queen to the stewards and then to the workers, enabling them to perform their tasks with purpose and direction. When everyone in the kingdom understands their role, it thrives. However, chaos may arise if the stewards do not grasp their responsibilities—if they fail to recognise the significance of their role and misinterpret or disregard the queen's instructions.

If the stewards begin to listen to the workers and act according to their wishes, the kingdom will not stand. Similarly, if the mind does not understand its role and allows external influences to dictate its actions, the individual's life will lose direction.

Every monarchy is powerful because those in power—the queen, the stewards, the governors—understand their authority.

At the same time, governments can falter in a matter of years due to instability and change. A kingdom, when properly structured, holds great power and authority.

You are a kingdom, representing a greater divine realm. Once you comprehend the role of your mind, its power, and its function in your life, you will realise just how crucial it is. Even in the most magnificent monarchy, if the workers neglect to follow the queen's directives and fail to execute the ultimate vision for the kingdom, the monarchy will crumble. Similarly, in your life, if you do not govern your mind with clarity and purpose, your greatness will remain stifled.

Your mind should only accept guidance from your spirit—from your beliefs, purpose, and the divine truth within you. The mind cannot be ruled by what is observed or felt in the physical realm, for the physical is limited. The physical world is rooted in what is fixed and present, like the clock ticking—precisely 10 minutes past 10, nothing more and nothing less. However, you, as a dynamic being, are not restricted to these fixed perceptions. You can shape your destiny beyond what is visible.

I urge you to believe, as you never have before, that you are magnificently created and destined for greatness. You are a remarkable man, a remarkable woman, or a remarkable child reading these words right now, and your greatness will undoubtedly come to pass because you are determined to transform your life from the inside out. Your journey of transformation begins within—by understanding and aligning your mind with your deepest beliefs, purpose, and calling.

Your mind is the gateway to your greatness. As you step through this gateway, you enter your future, a new life rich with greatness, majesty, and glory. Do not allow your present circumstances to dictate your future. Never permit the labels society places upon you to define your potential. The world may attempt to impose its limitations on you, but you must break free. Be transformed through the renewal of your mind.

Unlocking Greatness: The Power of the Spiritual Mind

Many were born into poverty from families experiencing extreme hardship. Dr. Myles Munroe, one of my greatest mentors and a transformational leader, was born under such circumstances. Raised in a one-bedroom home, sleeping on the floor with his siblings, he rose to become one of the greatest minds the world has ever known. He became a profound transformational leader and mentor, shaping countless lives and leaving behind a legacy that will impact generations. Dr. Munroe became a multi-millionaire, demonstrating that your current situation does not define who you are or who you will become.

So, who says that your current circumstances determine your destiny? Who tells you that your status defines your worth? Who claims that just because you find yourself in a foreign land, labelled as a "foreigner" or "asylum seeker," this defines you? These are merely temporary conditions, not permanent truths. Do not cling to these labels. Instead, embrace the truth of who you are—who God created you to be and who He believes you are.

Everything that will ever exist is contained within every seed. The potential is encoded in the seed, with its unique fingerprint indicating what it will become from the very start. The fruit is already within the seed. You don't need to look far to discover your greatness, for it resides within you. Before you were born, God created you with all the greatness you will ever need, encoding it into your very being. If He says you are great, that is the belief you must hold onto, and nothing less.

Change your beliefs now and prepare your mind to conceive what is unseen, intangible, and spiritual. Do not conceal your beliefs out of fear of what others may say. Do not hide them simply because they make you appear different. Open your mind to embrace your true potential. Prepare your mind to be spiritually guided and ensure it is ready to accept the seeds within it. Your mind must not suppress your greatness, passion, or power.

Your mind is the gateway through which your greatness will emerge. Regardless of your origin or current circumstances, a spiritually governed mind is vibrant. In contrast, a mind ruled by the physical realm is lifeless. If your mind is spiritually governed, you will ultimately breathe life into the greatness within you. The seed will thrive, just as an orange seed planted in fertile soil will sprout and produce oranges.

The Perils of Physical Governing

Now, let's consider the alternative: if you choose to be governed by the physical—by what you see, hear, feel, and touch—then the fruit you hold in your hand today, whether it be success, wealth, or status, cannot dictate the transformation of your life. If I place that orange fruit into fertile soil, it will cease to produce anything new. Over time, it will decay.

Fruit, as we know, is perishable. The physical world is perishable, and so are the things we observe. That is why God says, "I have come to give you life so that you might not perish but have eternal life." A life governed by the spirit—only a spiritually governed mind can foster life. The physical world is subject to change, and the fruits of this world will ultimately decay.

Do not look towards others and envy what they possess. Do not attempt to imitate others or desire to be like them. Look within yourself and uncover your greatness. Become the most authentic version of yourself; naturally, you will flourish into the remarkable person you were born to be. Do not allow the physical world to govern your mind. Everything you observe is subject to change.

You may have the best job in the world today—perhaps you are a company director or a CEO. But tomorrow, that job could be gone. You might find yourself redundant. What then? Will you lose your sense of self? Will you define your worth by the work you do or the job you hold? If you are struggling now, or your circumstances seem challenging, should you think you are worthless? No, that is not who you are. You possess tremendous value and an incredible purpose in this world.

Do not conform to the patterns of this world, but be transformed by the renewal of your mind. By doing so, you align yourself with your highest purpose— the great purpose that God has planned for you.

The physical world is subject to change. You may be poor today and wealthy tomorrow. In a week, you could become a millionaire. The stories of successful millionaires reveal this truth. They were once like you —filled with a dream and belief, but lacking the material wealth they now possess. They transformed their lives from within through the power of belief. And so can you.

The Power of Thought: The Roots of Your Beliefs

Once the soil is prepared, you can begin planting your seeds of greatness. These seeds represent your beliefs—the foundation of your potential. But just as a seed must send down roots to anchor itself in the soil, your beliefs must also establish roots to ground you in your purpose.

The first root, the taproot, is the deepest and most crucial. It anchors the plant in the soil, providing stability and nourishment. In your mind, the taproot represents your core conviction—the foundation of your thoughts. Your core conviction determines the direction of your life, shaping your perceptions, attitudes, and actions. If your core conviction is that you are destined for greatness, everything else will follow. Your secondary beliefs, thoughts, and actions will stem from this core conviction, just as the smaller roots emerge from the taproot.

Understanding your core conviction is essential for unlocking your greatness. If your core conviction is rooted in self-doubt or fear, your thoughts will be equally constrained. However, if they are grounded in confidence and possibility, your thoughts will evolve into positive actions that align with your greatness.

Never underestimate the power of your mind. Your thoughts and beliefs shape your destiny. Keep your mind focused on the spiritual, on the unseen, and trust that your beliefs will manifest in the physical world. Always remember that transformation begins from within, and that your garden, which is your mind, is sacred.

If you wish to witness the harvest of your potential—the fruits of your greatness—you must nurture it with care and devotion. You need to be selective about the thoughts you harbour in your mind. Your thoughts are the roots from which everything else will grow and be fed. If your thoughts are grounded in empowering beliefs, values, and possibilities, they will extend into strong branches, yielding the fruit of your dreams.

Your belief is the engine that drives everything. Your beliefs shape your thoughts, and your thoughts shape your actions. The actions you take will dictate the results you achieve. But all of this starts with belief. As you continue this journey, remember that your mind is the fertile soil where your dreams take root. Your beliefs are the seeds, and through the power of these beliefs, your greatness will be realised.

Protecting Your Mind and Safeguarding Your Greatness

> *"Your mind is a garden. Your thoughts are the seeds. The harvest can either be flowers or weeds."* – William Wordsworth.

Your mind is where every seed of greatness will be planted, nurtured, and eventually harvested. It's where you will grow into the person you were born to be—but it's also where your greatness can be destroyed if you allow literal and figurative pests to invade.

As much as you prepare the soil of your mind to receive the seeds of greatness, you must also protect it. As gardeners must guard their gardens and plants from pests, you must protect your mind and beliefs from negativity, doubt, and criticism. Today, we will look at how you can guard your mind from these destructive forces, ensuring that your seeds of greatness have the environment they need to thrive.

Let's take a moment to imagine a real garden where you've carefully sown the seeds of the fruits you wish to reap. Perhaps you've planted tomatoes. If the conditions are right—if the soil is fertile, the weather is favourable, and the seeds are nurtured—the tomato plant will thrive and eventually bear fruit. But, as with any garden, pests may also arrive. You might find insects, snails, slugs, or even rodents, which can potentially ruin the harvest. They could attack the fruits, the branches, or leaves, preventing your tomatoes from fully maturing and ripening for harvest.

Similarly, the seeds you plant in the garden of your mind—your beliefs and thoughts—possess the potential to flourish into greatness. However, just as pests can hinder a plant's growth, negative influences in your life—such as doubts, naysayers, or fears—can suppress your potential. These external forces can obstruct your greatness from manifesting. The seed will hold potential, never realising its full capabilities, much like a tomato seed that never bears fruit or ripens.

To truly become the person you are meant to be—a victor, a leader, a pioneer—you must cultivate the garden of your mind and defend it from any pests that could destroy your potential. Naysayers, pessimists, and anyone who doubts your dreams must be kept outside your garden. This is your sacred space, and only those who believe in your greatness and potential should be permitted entry.

The Power of Vigilance and Focus

To protect your mind, you must be vigilant. Be mindful of what you allow to enter your consciousness. The world is full of distractions and negative influences, and letting them take root in your mind is easy. But just as you would not let pests destroy your crops, you must not let negativity seep into your thoughts. Keep your mind sharp, and guard it from all intruders. Be conscious of the influences around you and deliberately shut out anything that doesn't serve your highest good and purpose.

The pessimist's voice is loud, always seeking to discredit your dreams and persuade you that your ideas are unattainable. Don't let them in. Shut out the negativity, the doubts, and the individuals who bring you down. Be intentional in safeguarding your garden, for it is here that your greatness will emerge. Your seed of greatness may be unknown to the world now, but we are about to uncover it through this journey. It's time to nurture and defend it fiercely.

You must take full ownership of your garden and your mind. If you want the seed of greatness to take root, you must ensure that no one and nothing is allowed to trespass into this space. Keep out the weeds of doubt, fear, and pessimism. You are the gardener of your mind, and you are in control of what grows within it. You cannot afford to let distractions, negativity, or obstacles impede the growth of your greatness.

As you progress on this journey to unlocking your greatness, remember the power of your mind. Just as a seed holds the potential to grow into a magnificent tree, your mind also harbours the potential for greatness. If you are an orange seed, it matters not if you are surrounded by trees that bear lemons, tangerines, grapefruits, or papayas. You needn't imitate them, nor should you feel insecure or pressured to conform. Instead, concentrate on your potential and on becoming who you were meant to be. Avoid looking around you. Rather, look deep within yourself to the source of your greatness. The soil in which your seed is planted is where your roots will grow. From here, your nourishment will flow, enabling you to develop and express the greatness within you.

Now, direct your undivided attention to your heart's deepest desires and dreams. Envision the ideal person you wish to become—the one who will bring you fulfilment, joy, peace, and rest, irrespective of what the world thinks or does. Focus solely on that vision, that image, that fruit you are destined to bear. Allow your mind to be receptive to your beliefs and thoughts. Make it fertile, and remain open to receiving only what will lead you towards greatness.

Do not harden your heart or your mind. You may not believe everything I've said, but remember your beliefs—not mine—will shape and determine who you become. So, ensure you get them right. Let your mind absorb only those beliefs that will deliberately and consciously shape you into the person you are meant to be. Open your mind to your vision and greatness, and step forward into your destiny as never before.

The journey to unlock your greatness begins internally—by transforming your beliefs and concentrating on your purpose. It has been a genuine honour to accompany you on this journey. I wish you a fulfilling, glorious, and exceptional life, leaving a lasting legacy for future generations.

DAY SEVEN

Unlocking the Gateway to Your Greatness

"Not everybody can be famous, but everybody can be great because greatness is determined by service."
–Martin Luther King Jr.

Welcome to day seven of your seven-day transformational journey towards unlocking your greatness with Dr. Sylvia Forchap Likambi. I am here to guide you through the final stage of your journey to greatness. You are destined for greatness, and nothing less than greatness will suffice. Your best is the only acceptable standard because you have been uniquely created by the divine and Almighty God to fulfil a remarkable mission that only you can accomplish. No one else can do it better than you.

So, come, arise, and join me as we embark on this final step of your journey to greatness. Today, we unlock your potential, open the door, and allow it to step out into the world, for today marks the occasion when your greatness will no longer be kept inside but revealed to all. I am so excited for you because today is the day, we unleash that greatness.

Today, we will place the key into the door that has confined your greatness. That door, which has kept you shackled to a life of average mediocrity, will open, and your greatness will boldly step forth, ready to be seen by everyone.

Welcome on board, Day Seven! Seven is a powerful number; it signifies completion — the end of one era and the beginning of a new one. In seven days, we have completed the process of sowing and nurturing your greatness. Now, we enter a new era where you will walk in your greatness daily. So, let us jump in together, enthusiastically and passionately, to unlock this door that has kept your greatness trapped and hidden for too long.

Now, allow me to take you on a mental journey. I would like you to envision a home and a door. I enjoy utilising mental images and metaphors as they assist you in feeling and experiencing what I am discussing. These metaphors render what I'm saying tangible and real so you can truly embrace it. I want you to see with your own eyes, to perceive it in your way—not as I perceive it, but in a manner that makes sense to you. It's your perception that shapes your reality—not mine. Your perception is the key that unlocks the door to your greatness, and it is your key to the future you desire. The lock will either confine you to your current situation or allow you to step forward into your destiny.

Now, picture a home. There is a door to the outside, and inside the home, there is a corridor that leads to all the different parts of the house—the kitchen, the dining room, the living room, the bedroom, and so on. Imagine that you are in this home, relaxed and at peace. Perhaps it is night, and you are sleeping in your room. You don't know what is happening outside; there could be war, violence, or people fighting. You cannot see any of it because you are in your safe, secure home, your sanctuary. The door to your home is shut, and no one can enter unless you allow them to. Anyone who enters without your permission—through a broken window or by forcing the door open—is a thief and has no right to be there. They have no say in who you are or who you are becoming.

Now, you hold the key to that door—the key to your mind. This is where transformation occurs. That door represents your mind, and the transition takes place when you give someone or something the authority to enter your life or leave it. When you allow yourself to step outside your home, you do so confidently, knowing you are not a thief. You open the door boldly, without fear, because you are ready. Similarly, when someone knocks at your door, you open it because you are prepared to welcome them.

This door is the gateway—the mind is the gateway. It is the place where the transformation occurs. Today, we will open it and allow it to birth your greatness—like a seed breaking through the ground as a shoot and revealing its true essence and nature to the world (the tree and the fruit within). Once you understand how to access the gateway to your greatness in your mind, you will realise the great power that lies within. Similarly, when you know the transformational power of your thoughts and beliefs, you will truly see how great and magnificent you are. This realisation will set you free to finally live the life you were born and called to live.

True freedom is not about escaping physical prisons—prisons built and guarded by man. No! True freedom comes when you break free from the prison of your mind. You have been living in captivity because you have locked the door to your mind, trapping your potential within. You've stayed inside, believing you are not ready to step out. You have told yourself that you are immature, not good enough, inadequate, or that the world is not ready for you. So, you kept the door locked, convinced you had nothing of value to offer.

But today, we are unlocking that door. It is time to stop hiding in the shadows of self-doubt and step into the light of your greatness. The world is waiting for you. Your greatness is ready to be revealed. All you need to do is unlock that door—unlock your mind, and walk boldly into the future you've always dreamed of.

You may be saying, "Dr Sylvia, you must be joking. I'm not good enough. The world isn't ready to see me as I am." Or, "I'm such a mess; the world is unprepared for my mess yet." You then continue to lock the door to your greatness and remain trapped in what you perceive as a mess forever. But when you decide, "No matter what the world says, it doesn't matter. I am going to open this door. I am ready, mess and all, in my current situation, circumstance, and condition," the transformation begins.

It is your decision. You hold the key to that door. If you don't open it, no one else can. No one can rescue you—not even God. He has already given you the key. That's why He says that your will is your greatest power. If He could, He would make all your choices for you, but He doesn't. He allows you to make them yourself. He has granted you a sovereign will and authority over the key that unlocks the door to your greatness. This key will open the door to your future, to the life you were born and destined to live.

Now, consider that door. Will you open it to anyone who knocks, even if you know they intend to cause you harm? Picture yourself standing there as a thief knocks on your door. You recognise they're dangerous, perhaps armed with a weapon, intending to kill or destroy you. Would you open that door? Of course not! You would retreat to your safe place—your bedroom, sanctuary, and refuge—and seek help from a greater authority and power.

Consider your home as your body and your room as your spirit—the essence of who you are, where the divine connection dwells. Spirit connects only with spirit. Being a spirit, God can only be related to through the spirit. When you recognise that your room—your spirit—is a safe haven, you can find solace in knowing it is secure. Regardless of what occurs outside—be it a storm or chilly weather—your home remains warm. Within, you are sheltered, shielded from the severity of the elements. The world may be turbulent, but you find peace within your home.

Your spirit is your sanctuary. Those who dwell in the presence of the Most High find refuge in the spirit of God within them. They are secure and protected in His spirit, remaining unaffected by external forces. Therefore, the question is: Will you open the door to any destructive influence from outside? Are you going to allow negativity, doubt, or criticism to enter? I would wager not.

Those external forces represent people who are quick to tell you that you're not good enough or a failure. They might say things like, "Look at your life —you don't have a job," or, "You're just an asylum seeker." These people are the ones who label you, but you don't need to allow them in. They are entitled to their opinions, but you cannot permit them to shape your reality. We cannot change certain things—like these people—because they are not meant to be altered by us. However, what we require is the serenity to live peacefully alongside them or, if necessary, apart from them.

These people come to teach you a very important life lesson—they come to help you understand that they do not have the power to define who you are or who you will become. You are the one who determines that. You decide who you become, and you decide who you indeed are.

So, I urge you to keep every naysayer out of your life. This could include your mother, your teacher, your father, or any close relative. Sometimes, those closest to us—our families—are the ones who hold us back. They may see us for who we are, and because they share our background, they might think, "We come from low-income families. We've never been to school. We're village children. How dare we dream big?" They ridicule you, laugh at your aspirations, and tell you to stop being a dreamer.

The people closest to you—your family—will often try to extinguish your dream. They'll tell you to stop because they only see your current reality. They don't understand the vision within you. They know the present, not the potential.

Be cautious. Be mindful of whom you allow in. Consider who you open the door to. Are they there to encourage or discourage you? Anyone who discourages you does not aid in your journey to becoming the remarkable person you are destined to be, so do not let them in. You must not conform to their limitations. The greatness within you should transform you by renewing your mind and thoughts with the understanding of your potential and purpose.

Imagine you're at home now, enjoying a peaceful night's sleep while the storm rages outside. People are rushing for shelter, getting drenched in the rain, perhaps even arguing. Yet, you're at peace in your home, oblivious to the chaos beyond. But when you open that door, you step out of your safe haven into the world. And because you know the warmth, tranquillity, and care of your home, you venture out prepared, clad, nourished, and ready to face the journey ahead.

So, will you open that door now? The key is in your mind. The doorway represents your mind. Will you unlock it and allow your greater self to enter the world? It is time for you to walk boldly through that door. Your greatness awaits, and the world is ready for you. The key is yours—open the door and step into your destiny.

Once and for all, be liberated, be free. Stop being a slave to yourself. Stop standing in your own way on the journey to greatness. Open the door to your soul and to your greatness today! Do not be afraid. Whether or not the world is ready to embrace your greatness is none of your concern and shouldn't trouble you. Do not fear their judgments, be it that they think you're different or don't belong. Step forth and reveal yourself to the world just as you are, in your greatness, authenticity, and fullness.

If you were ever unsure about the seed you were about to sow, let everything I've shared with you today assure you that this is the final stage. You should now be confident in your walk. Know that walking forward with certainty—knowing you are wonderful and deeply rooted in that understanding—will keep you unwavering.

When you walk out with certainty, you are grounded in that source—you know what it's like to dwell in the spirit. You experience the joy, the peace, and the fulfilment that comes from being fully aligned with who you are—the spirit within. This inner certainty will keep you rooted. When the world becomes harsh, when you lose your job, and when things fall apart, this certainty will remind you that you are remarkable. Remember, you are destined for greatness. You are a victor, a creator. That truth will keep you grounded, not opinions or feelings.

So, are you ready now? Are you prepared to open that door? Are you ready for the world to see your greatness—the greatness that you embody? Are you prepared to make that reality visible so the world can acclimatise to it? You must speak life into who you are becoming. You must decree and declare your future, and so it shall be.

Whether they celebrate you or envy you, it does not matter. Your greatness is unstoppable. The world can accept or reject it, but that will never change who you are or the path you follow. Prepare yourself now, open that door, and step outside. You are great, and nothing can hold you back.

Forget about the petty, limiting mindsets that judge you by your skin colour, race, gender, or disability. These factors do not define you, and they never will.

God is a God of variety. The colour of your skin, whether brown, black, white or any shade in between, exists for a reason and a purpose. Be confident in your complexion. Be confident in your colour. I am a black woman speaking to you, but I do not define myself solely by my gender or the colour of my skin. Yet, I am unapologetically black and a woman, proud of my colour and identity.

I show up with dignity, pride, and grace when I step into the world. I walk with my head held high, fully aware that God made me this colour for a reason. I am proud of my melanin—it is a gift that provides me with natural protection from the sun, and I am grateful for it. My skin shields and nourishes me, offering protection from harm. I do not need to tan or seek out harmful rays; I am already beautifully and naturally tanned.

How glorious are the works of His hands! He created me in His image, and the spirit that resides within me is the spirit of the Almighty. No racial prejudice or ignorance can diminish or break me. No one can prevent me from being who I am meant to be.

In the same manner, you must step forth boldly into your greatness. Walk with conviction, fully embracing who you are and who you were born to become. Regardless of your appearance, skin colour, race, background, or gender, you don't need permission from anyone. You don't need others to like your appearance or approve of you. You must walk unapologetically in your authenticity, allowing the world to see you for who you are. Whether they are pleased with it or not, that's their issue, not yours.

You are a light meant to shine brightly. If your light makes others uncomfortable or is too bright, allow them to move or wear a veil over their eyes to shield themselves from your radiance. But never, ever dim your light to please others or to make them comfortable while presenting a lesser and average version of yourself. Doing so risks settling for mediocrity, working beneath your greatness.

You are opening this door because you are ready. You have made a decision; you now understand who you are. You recognise the life you desire—one that brings you love, peace, satisfaction, joy, and inner contentment. You are aware of your power to exercise self-control. You now realise that it is not the actions or opinions of others that determine how you feel or respond, but rather who you are and the values and convictions you hold. You alone are responsible for your responses and reactions to the world around you. Your response is rooted in your identity, which enables you to step boldly and majestically into your future.

So, if you are ready, unlock this door now. You are awakening from your slumber. You are about to embark on your journey, step into your greatness, and embrace the transformation that awaits you. This is the transition point—when the seed sprouts from the soil. Make the decision now. A seed that remains in the soil and never breaks through to the surface will never bear fruit. Likewise, your greatness will not come to fruition unless you take action. You must unlock your potential, just as the seed of an orange tree sprouts, eventually growing into a tree that produces fruit.

Once you leave that door, those who recognise your potential will see who you are becoming. This is your time. Make no apologies, make no excuses—this is who you are. No matter where you come from or your situation, if you are not ready yet, go back and reread the previous days… You must be convinced there is no turning back once you open this door.

When you open the door, you allow the world to see you as you are. While inside your home, they cannot know if you are present, how many people are there, or what stage of your journey you are at. But once the door is open, they can see you. While they may not treat you as you deserve, that should not concern you. This journey is about unlocking your greatness, not anyone else's. You can never unlock the greatness of another person. This is a transformational journey—your journey. Only you hold the key to your life. Only you can unlock your mind and transform yourself by continually renewing your thoughts and beliefs.

When you know your beliefs are rooted in solid ground, on the rock of your Creator, you become unshakeable. You are grounded in your core convictions, which guide your purpose. Your purpose determines how you plan and live your life each day, always striving to become the great person you are destined to be. You do not turn to the left or the right; you do not seek to please others or to fit in. You live your purpose to the fullest, knowing you have one mission—to live a grand and glorious life honouring your Creator.

Your purpose will ultimately be fulfilled and leave a lasting legacy. Are you ready? Have you envisioned the life you desire? Have you internalised that vision? Have you written it down? If you haven't, remember, if you do not take action, someone else will shape that vision for you.

Now, open the door. Walk boldly into your greatness. From this point on, you will no longer need to unlock your greatness, for it has already been revealed and set free. You have entered a new phase: a life where your greatness is unleashed, and you walk in it daily.

A Personal Moment of Realisation

As I write this, my baby is knocking at the door, wanting me to open it. This moment is so timely. I am in my bedroom upstairs, working quietly, and she's crying, wishing to come in. She needs me. She's wonderful, beautiful, and innocent. But until I open the door, she cannot enter. She cannot benefit from what I have to give her—my love, my nurturing, and my care. She cannot receive the gifts that only I can offer as her mother unless I open that door.

This moment serves as the perfect metaphor. Just as I must open the door for her to enter so I can care for her, you, too, must open the door to the greatness within you. You must step forward and allow the world to experience your gifts. Keeping the door closed serves no one. By unlocking it, you give the world access to the brilliance that lies within you.

Therefore, if you are still fearful and doubtful, I want you to know that I am right here with you. More importantly, your Creator is with you every step of the way. He is the ultimate source of your greatness. He knows your purpose and has placed that desire in your heart. He is there to guide you. Do not be afraid. Step boldly through that door, knowing He is with you and will always be with you.

As you move forward, there will be challenges, but remember, you are rooted. Your roots are deep, and no storm can uproot you. You are destined for greatness. You have an amazing journey ahead of you—an unapologetic journey into your greatness. Good luck. As you embrace your greatness, the world will recognise the true you—the fearless, brave, and courageous person you were always meant to be. You are a conqueror, a victor, a masterpiece. Go forth and fulfil your purpose.

You've been on this incredible journey with your transformation friend and coach, Dr Sylvia Forchap-Likambi. It's been a true honour and privilege to take you through your authentic and divine journey of unlocking your greatness and living a fulfilled, glorious, and purpose-driven life. Enjoy your journey and the ride! Thank you for trusting me and walking with me.

With immense love and gratitude,
Dr Sylvia Forchap-Likambi

ABOUT THE AUTHOR

Dr Sylvia Forchap-Likambi

Dr. Sylvia Forchap-Likambi is a visionary, multi-award-winning leading empowerment and transformation authority, transformational Speaker, Coach, and eight-time international best-selling author; specialised in the delivery of very high quality/cutting-edge empowerment and revolutionary leadership and transformation programs. She is the Founder and Global Chair of The Global Visionary Women Network, Founder and CEO of "Behaviour Changed" Award Winning Community Interest Company, Voice of Nations; and Global CEO/Consultant of Dr Sylvia Likambi International/ Dr Sylvia Likambi International Health & Wellbeing Clinic.

Over the years, she has coached, empowered, inspired, and positively impacted/ transformed over 1.5 million lives globally, thousands of female entrepreneurs, and relentlessly empowered many to come out of addictions, depression, get into training, volunteering, employment/

self-employment, leadership roles; and also offered them several of such opportunities through her organizations.

She grew up in Cameroon, and later moved to Italy where she earned a Doctor of Pharmacy degree and a PhD degree. She was awarded the Italian Ministry of Higher Education and Research scholarship for excellence, and the Australian- Europe Scholarships to accomplish a year's collaboration with the University of Sydney (Nepean Hospital). At completion of her PhD in Australia and Italy, she worked as Postdoctoral Researcher in Italy and the UK; and became Honorary Research Associate with the Royal Liverpool University Hospital in 2008, and a member of The European Hematology Association in 2009.

Dr Sylvia has participated immensely in leukaemia research and is author/co-author in a number of international peer reviewed journals. She is also an ILM certified executive and business/Life Coach and a bestselling author. She was nominated in the African Business Chamber's UK TOP 100 African Business Leaders and Entrepreneurs 2022 and 2024 Lists, and listed on the Top 25 Black Entrepreneurs To Watch in 2021 by The UK Black Business Show. She was also the winner of Honorary Award for Exemplary Professional Leadership Recognition at the Enterprise Minds Awards 2018, The Positive Role Model for Gender Award at The UK National Diversity Awards 2016, and multiple nominee/ finalist for

Mentoring Champion of the Year at The SEN Powerful Together Awards 2012-2014, and The Member's Choice Awards in 2012 and 2013 (which celebrates the achievements of an individual who can demonstrate their commitment and contribution to the world of social enterprise, and critically, how they have enabled entrepreneurs to achieve their goals and aspirations).

She brings a very unique and dynamic blend of inspiration, purpose, empowerment, and transformation in her mentoring, coaching, and engagements; that has the potential of transforming the most dormant/negative mindset into a highly productive/positive and dynamic mindset, capable of setting and achieving any life goal.

She is a strong believer of the fact that as leaders we are called to serve rather than being served, and that to whom much is given much is expected. As a result, she endlessly embarks on a selfless journey of service and giving back to her community without an expectation of being financially rewarded or praised. Her greatest reward is in the satisfaction she gets from experiencing lives being transformed as a result of her humble service to humanity.

Her ethnicity, life experiences, educational background, resilient nature, and down to earth personality has given her the tremendous opportunity and privilege to serve and interact with some of the most deprived and underprivileged within diverse cultures, educational backgrounds, and communities; inspiring and challenging them to step forth confidently to unleash their untapped potentials and fulfil their dreams, regardless of their background, gender or circumstances.

She has also delivered several successful and life transforming revolutionary leadership, empowerment programs for VON (leading it to earn the prestigious SEN Behaviour Changed Award in 2013), WEA, and a host of commissioned projects nationally and internationally.

Dr Sylvia's life is true testament of her authority and leadership; she's a power wife and power mum to three incredibly gifted and talented children who are some of the world's and our nation's youngest authors of multiple books.

She has featured on several national and international Radio and TV stations, to speak on the theme of female empowerment, entrepreneurship, leadership, and other topics; and been guest/ keynote speaker to several audiences, ranging from community groups to universities.

About The Publisher

Likambi Global Publishing Ltd

Email: enquiries@likambiglobalpublishing.com

Tel: +44 (0) 7539 216072

www.likambiglobalpublishing.com

We are a Dynamic Family-Led Cutting-Edge Global Publisher set up to simplify and enhance your writing and publishing experience and unique journey to becoming a renowned and confident author.

Whether you are an adult or child, we have a special team that is devoted to working with you throughout your writing and publishing journey with us! All of our consultants and coaches/mentors are bestselling authors with years of hands-on experience and a wealth of knowledge uniquely tailored to meet your individual needs!

Our goal is to provide you with the ultimate writing and publishing experience required to share your unique message and voice as an author with the world and strive to greater heights!

Publications are done three times a year; January, June, and November. All manuscripts must be received at least 90 days prior to publication dates.

www.ingramcontent.com/pod-product-compliance
Lightning Source LLC
Chambersburg PA
CBHW050255120526
44590CB00016B/2364